JOY

YOU ARE THE NEW WORLD

www.unionofloveandlight.com

RECEIVED BY JENNIFER STARLIGHT

Joshua Books

P.O. Box 5149, Maroochydore BC
Queensland Australia 4558

All correspondence to the publisher
at the above address.

Master Distribution by: Joshua Books

ISBN 0-9757953-0-9

Category: New Age: Channelled Works: Author

Joshua Books
www.joshuabooks.com

Jennifer Starlight's 'Union' is an extraordinary document which presents the initial series of beautiful and powerful teachings from 'The Union of Love and Light'. It is also an important foundation for the second series of teachings which follows in 'Joy'.

"This Truth will resonate on a very deep level if you are ready and if you are not... know that your heart will seek out our message when you and your mind have had enough of the illusion that is now so dense on your planet.

It is our greatest honour to now assist and guide you on the greatest journey of exploration of which any soul, in any time, could experience. We are the 'Union of Love and Light' and we have no demands. Our communion with you is our greatest joy and highest purpose".

To dear Matthew –
Wishing you joy
all-ways!

Jennifer '11

FOREWORD

'Joy' is the second channelled work in a series that I have been privileged to receive, and these communions with the Union of Love and Light continue to be intense and rewarding experiences.

In allowing myself to feel and absorb these teachings during channelling, denied and deeply held emotions were finally acknowledged, and 'roadblocks' on my own journey of self-discovery were removed. The simple act of acknowledging these emotions was often a challenge, but the divine gift they offered was always a joyous discovery.

Many aspects of humanity continue to exist within the fog of illusion and the paralysis of fear, and I believe that only through an aching desire for the truth, and the meaning it brings to our very existence, can we create a New World of love and light for our 'future ancestors' – our children!

Allow yourself to receive and cherish the infinite love and universal truths this Spiritual Brethren so passionately and joyfully wish to share with each and every heart. Know they are pleading with us to awaken and return to the sacredness of our own being, for only then shall we discover the love and peace for which we have been searching.

To my father, Jim Walpole and our Spiritual Brother, Darion, I give my deepest love and gratitude, for their mutual dedication and determination has allowed all those involved, seen and unseen, to bring 'Joy' to the world.

Jennifer Starlight

CONTENTS

Introduction. 15

Message from Father Time. 18

Time Release Exercise 21

The Rose Red Ray 'Shalamar' 25

Masters, Guides and Angels 27

The Message of Metatron. 30

Your Universe – A Divine Consciousness 32

Temple of the Moon 34

The Earth 36

Dedication to the Mother of all Nature. 39

The Moon 42

Mercury 45

Temple of the Sun. 50

Venus 52

The Sun. 54

Mars. 60

Temple of the Stars 62

Jupiter 64

Saturn. 68

Uranus 71

Neptune & Pluto. 75

The Grand Cycle of Service. 77

Beyond the Light 'Darion' 83

The Sacred Journey of the Black and White Rays 89

Shades of Grey 92

Re-union Exercise of Heart, Mind and Soul 96

River of Stars. 99

Revelations. 103

The Circle of Life. 106

The Mystery and the Majesty. 110

The Ten Commitments 114

The Crystal Ball 116

Message of the Star Elders 120

The Activation of the Ten Commitments 127

The Meditator. 130

The Star and the Stone. 133

Appendix A – Your Tree of Diamonds .137

Appendix B – The Sacred Equation. 161

The Author of 'Union' and 'Joy' 170

CONTENTS

ILLUSTRATIONS

Time Release Exercise 23

Planets & Numbers Associated with each Diamond Light. 44

Planets & Temples of the Diamond Light System 48

Infinite Braids of Light. 58

Sacred Chambers of the Sun 59

Union of Sacred Darkness & Divine Light. 84

Hueman Path of Union 88

Re-Union Exercise of Heart, Mind and Soul 96

The Ten Commitments 126

JOY

For my beloved
Gregory.

A LIGHT WILL SHINE UPON

THEE, LIKE NO OTHER

THOU HAST KNOWN,

WHERE ALL GREAT

KINGDOMS WILL JOIN AS

ONE IN BROTHERHOOD,

TO SERVE IN UNIFICATION

FOR PEACE ON EARTH

THE UNION OF LOVE AND LIGHT

Jennifer Starlight

AUTHOR'S NOTES

'Diamond Lights' – The concept of the Diamond Lights is central to the teachings presented in my first channelled work 'Union - A Guide to the New World', and as they remain essential elements in 'Joy', it is important to re-state the fundamental principles of those teachings for readers who may not have access to the first publication. (See Appendix A, page 137)

'Hueman' – Uncommon spelling used throughout this work was introduced during channelling of 'Union'. The following excerpt from a message by the Spiritual Elders of Uluru:

'We have been the keepers and protectors of the Great Mother Snake, the Rainbow Mother of All Nature. She now coils around all her Creation to bring it back into the One Heart and the One Soul. Be in Union with your Soul by first being in Union with your Earth. Be in union with your Heart by being in Union with the Rainbow Mother of All Nature'.

'Hueman': Hue (Rainbow) – Man (**M**other of **A**ll **N**ature)

'**Scription**' – Introduced during channelling of 'Union':

'We, the Union of Love and Light have created this word to help you understand the energy behind the teachings. A Scription is a sacred writing of Light, and if you choose to follow the precise interpretations of the English language: A Script or Scripture is a system of writing or sacred text. An 'Ion' is an electrically charged atom or group of atoms that, when discharged, creates 'Lightning".

AUTHOR'S NOTE

14

INTRODUCTION

Greetings, dear ones. We, the Union, come forth to you once more in Love and Light. We walk by your side, we share your pain, we share your laughter, we share every facet of your being. We wish you to understand and know this now, for in conscious Union with us, in conscious Union with the One, shall you find the Peace, the Love, the Faith and the Truth which you have been looking for, so desperately. And when you find these things of which we speak, you shall also find your JOY, through the discovery, through the Union, through the Love and the Light.

Many of you stand on the edge of what appears as a very precarious cliff. You know you can't turn back, for to turn back is to go back into the illusion, into the fog, into the distance. But before you, we understand that all you can see is an Abyss, a great Void, the Unknown. This place where you stand now, this edge of the illusion and the reality, is an ominous place indeed for any Soul to experience. However, deep in your Soul, if you stop and listen, you shall realise that your Soul has travelled long and hard to come to this edge, to come to this place of the Unknown. For this is where your Soul has been birthed, this is the point of Creation, of Union, of God/Goddess/All That Is, and it is the way back home to the ONE HEART.

We would wish to liken this experience of standing on the edge to other times in your life experience where you could not see your way clear to make a decision, you could not see the wood for the trees, you could not see the Truth through the illusion.

You have had, if you cast your minds back, many similar experiences of a lesser degree, shall we say, and when you look back now on those experiences you realise that everything was in perfect chaos, in a perfect place of time and space. For, as you reflect on these experiences, many unforeseen things happened. There was a twist in the road, a corner to turn, a leap of faith to take. This, dear ones, is the journey of your Souls, and to this point you have taken these steps, you have had these experiences to bring you now to the greatest 'Leap of Faith' that any Soul could experience. For when you step off the edge, you shall instantaneously find your wings, feel your Heart, and know your Soul. And in that Grand Divine Moment so shall you have Union with All That Is, and all fear, illusion, doubt and distrust shall leave you, shall dissolve back into its original form of Love and Light.

So, in the following Scriptions, we wish to give you support with Love, with Faith and with Truth to guide you, and to assist you in the leap that only you and your Divine Will can make. For when you take that leap, you shall experience true Joy, and true Oneness.

Your Souls have been aching for this moment. Your Souls have travelled long and hard. It is your Soul's future, it is your Soul's awakening that this leap shall bring. For understand, in a sense, this life you lead is a dream and your Soul is the dreamer. You may choose in another way to call your Soul your Higher Self, for in Truth that is what it is. Your Soul has orchestrated the dreams, so from your Soul has been birthed this experience, this dream that you now walk through on your Earthly plane.

This has been required by your Soul, this has been created by your Soul, and we wish you to understand, at this point, because it is a dream does not necessarily mean it is an illusion, for when you remember and understand that this life is a reflection of the Highest Consciousness of your Soul, you will understand the purpose that it is serving. It is only when you do not realise that this dream that you walk and experience is something else, other than what you call your reality, that is when you create illusion. For, in reality you are not this dream, in reality you are the dreamer, you are the Higher Self, you are the Higher Consciousness that has chosen to experience another way of growth, another way of play, another way of experiment. So understand, this experiment, this experience, is a Divine process, a very important process in the expansion of the Soul.

We shall be bringing you new information, and we shall be exploring even further your Hueman bodies, your Earth and your Universe, for you are about to awaken from a very long dream and we wish you to be prepared fully, lovingly and wisely. It is the New World that you will awaken to, and there will be no sleepwalkers, there will be no nightmares, and there will be no unconscious choices. You shall be fully awake, you shall be fully aware, you shall be fully adjusted, and you shall fully embody the Divine Being that you have always been. So, dear ones, as you stand at the edge of the Abyss, at the edge of the New World, the new way, the only way, understand in essence and in Truth, it is time for you to jump for JOY!

MESSAGE FROM
FATHER TIME

We the Union of Love, and we, the Union of Light, bring you, with great honour and great reverence, the presence of what you may wish to call the Father of Time. Please listen to his message with your Heart and your Soul, and be willing to embrace all that is going to be conveyed to you, for it is of utmost importance that you understand the message, as well as its intention.

Here I am with you now, and here I shall be with you forever. Your challenges to this point have been many and varied, and your gifts to this point have been beautiful and more importantly, often misunderstood. You have arrived, all of you now, at a point in time and in space that will allow you an opportunity, not seen before in your Hueman history. For, understand firstly, before you can fully embrace this opportunity, there are only two points of reference when I speak of time. There is NOW and there is THEN. NOW is the Eternal One Moment, THEN can either be your past or future perception of time and space. You must forget the THEN *you have* experienced and the THEN *you wish* to experience. For all opportunities can only be embraced in the NOW.

I, the Father of Time, do not exist THEN, I can only exist NOW, as you do. The THEN that I speak of is also what *you perceive* as the dream, however, the dream is just a projection of your Soul's desire. It is only the perception of that dream by the ego and by the mind that creates illusion. I am not asking you to change your mind, I am asking you to change your perception. And I am not asking you to change the desire of your Soul and the projection of its dream, I am asking you to fully embrace it NOW. For understand, the Soul's projection of its desire, of its dream, can only be experienced in the NOW. This brings much difficulty to the mind and its ego. For the mind and the ego prefer to stay in the perception of the THEN, whether it be past or future.

Up to this point in your Hueman history you have required the THEN, but, in the process, you have actually turned your back on the NOW. This has caused a split in the Union of your Heart and Soul with your Mind and Ego. These must be brought back into alignment for you to experience the NOW, and not to be trapped in the THEN. Many of you, in your Hueman minds and your Hueman bodies have locked within them many experiences from the past THEN, with much anticipation also around the future THEN. Many waste the NOW moment perceiving their lives as: "Back THEN I wasn't happy, but when I do, or get, such and such, THEN I will be happy". By doing this, you have disregarded and denied the NOW.

For in this dream you walk, the only place your nightmares can exist are in the THEN, in the reflection, and in the perception of all that's behind you, and before you. Put another way, much of your energy is locked in "time capsules" that do not exist in the NOW. Many run in fear from their past, and carry it into their future. This, of course, brings the reflection and perception of the nightmare, of having no control, of having no comfort, of having no safety. For the true dream of the Soul always exists in the present moment.

In Truth, the nightmare which, in essence, is the illusion, can only exist in the THEN moment. There is no illusion in the NOW moment. When your Mind, Heart and Soul are in Union, you will be in the NOW, you will be in the JOY. You will be in your Power, in your Truth, and in your Divine Being.

I, Father Time, I have the job of releasing you from your chains of restriction, by helping you understand what they are to begin with. So I, Father Time, like my brother the Angel Lucifer, the one you call Fear, have both sacrificed our expansion, to show you the restrictions within your Times of Fear, and your Fears of Time. However, as I am sure you are realising, my brother and I are returning back into the ONE HEART, so I now come forth to tell you, in Love and support, that I shall be releasing myself from your Dimension, and from your perception. I wish for your blessing, and I wish for your Will to release me from your body and your mind, for we are all going Home, we are all returning back into the freedom of our Spirits, of our Divine Essence.

Many of you would already be experiencing timelessness in your daily lives, even confusion about what day it may be. How quickly the years are going, you are saying, time is speeding up, you are saying. I have no time NOW to do all the things I should have done THEN! If you are fully present in the NOW moment, you will have more time and more space, and more ease for your daily journey, than you can possibly imagine. I, Father Time, along with you, need release NOW from these restrictions, the illusions of the past, and the illusions of the future.

I wish now to share with you a visual exercise that will assist in my release from your minds and your bodies. For understand, your Heart and your Soul are not constrained by time, and they are not constrained by space. However your minds and your bodies are constrained, so for the purpose of this exercise, I would like you to find a quiet space, a peaceful space, a space where you shall not be disturbed.

TIME RELEASE EXERCISE

1. I ask you *now* to gently close your eyes, and bring your awareness to the tip of your nose.

2. Take a few minutes to focus on your breath, and as you breathe in, see yourself breathing in pure Love and pure Light, and as you breathe out, also breathe out pure Love and pure Light.

3. As you continue to do this, bring your awareness to the **Five Diamond Light** of your Heart, and the **Four Diamond Light** of your Soul. See these two areas begin to fill with this pure Love, and this pure Light. Allow your Heart and Soul to awaken fully, and allow them to anchor you in the present NOW moment.

4. Visualise the figure 8 of Infinity joining these two Sacred Centres of the Heart and the Soul, and see this figure 8 also made of pure Love and pure Light, begin to gently pulse and spiral around your Heart and your Soul.

5. Allow that Love and Light to emanate from these two Centres, and fill your whole body. See it radiate out further into your Shell of Light, (your Auric Field) until your entire being is filled with this Light.

6. *Now* visualise a grid around your Shell of Light. See this web, this grid, as I, Father Time, the one that has kept you constrained, confined and restricted in my Love and my Light for you. See and feel your Shell of Light and your body become brighter, lighter, and radiate in Love.

7. In your mind's eye, see this 'grid of time' begin to melt, and be absorbed into the Love and Light now radiating from your Heart and Soul.

8. Then visualise your Shell of Light exploding and expanding, and radiating out as far as your imagination will allow. For you are all things, you are all Universes, and you are the Hearts and the Souls of All Existence.

9. Remain in this state of pure Love, Light, and expansion for as long as you choose, and when you return yourself to the NOW, see the figure 8 that brings your Heart and Soul into Union. See it turn into an Infinity symbol of Golden Light that will remain deeply within and around these Diamond Lights. Allow your Shell of Light to resume its normal form, and know that you have released me, the Father of Time, from the gridlock of your minds and your bodies, and most importantly from the illusion of THEN.

You may repeat this Time Release Exercise whenever you feel the illusion of THEN upon you. With endless Love, and timeless Light, be at peace and Joy in this infinite NOW!

TIME RELEASE EXERCISE

THE ROSE RED RAY 'SHALAMAR'

We, the Union of Love and the Union of Light, that is you, that is All, we now wish to bring forward to your awareness a Being of great Light. A Being beyond your Universe, a Being *almost* beyond your comprehension, a Being that will ignite the Light of Love deep within the Sacred Chamber of your Hearts. For this Being is our Spiritual Brethren, our Brother, our Sister, our Beloved. This, of whom we speak, is Shalamar.

It is with the greatest of Love, the greatest of Light, and the greatest remembrance of you, that I now come, I now speak, and I now share what is required for each Heart to remember, to receive and to rejoice. I, Shalamar, am part of this Group Consciousness of Union, this Group Consciousness of Love, and this Group Consciousness of Light. And I, like you, have been sent by the Source of All Love to reflect the Truth, the Joy and the Knowledge that is within each of us, no matter what our form, no matter what our colour, shape, size or belief system, and no matter what we think we are or are not. This, as you know, in its concept, is extremely clear and very simple, however, to remember this fact is one of the greatest challenges, not only for Hueman beings but also for many different forms in many different Dimensions. So do not fear that you are alone with this challenge, with this struggle of remembrance, with this separateness from Joy.

I, Shalamar, I am a Guardian of your Hearts, and it is my greatest gift to you, and it is my greatest Love for you that I wish to fuel the flame within; to re-awaken your Joy, your passion and your peace. Understand, peace, as you may have come to perceive it, is not a subtle energy by any means. Peace is the very foundation of passion, of purpose and of play. For it is only with the foundation of peace that you can ever begin to experience the Truth of passion, for peace is the portal to the Realm of your passion, and only from the expression of your passion can you experience your Joy. For Love is peace, and when fuelled by the flame of your Life Force, it is peace that allows your passion to burn, and to release your Joy into full expression.

Your colour Red has many aspects to it, many vibrations, many tones and even sounds associated with it. I wish you to know me through the Red Ray of your Rose, for this is how I physically manifest my expression to you, through the colour vibration of Rose Red, the Rose Red Ray of Manifestation.

I have walked your Earth as king and pauper. I have experienced your Earth in Love and darkness. I have lost my faith and regained my trust over many lifetimes. For how could I be here with you *now* without the inner *know*ing of the experience of the Hueman condition in which you brave Hearts find yourselves. That is also why the Rose Red Ray is an important expression of my essence, for Red is your earth, Red is your blood, Red is your richness. Red is your vitality, Red is your energy, your very Life Force, and Red is also your anger, your frustration and your fear.

The Rose is your beauty, your softness, your delicate Heart, your expression of Love, and your Sacred Mother. I come to you as the blood, as the Love, as the Masculine Force of Life, and the Feminine Flow of Love. In the Scriptions ahead, I shall be bringing you new concepts and Ancient Truths, and I shall share parts of your history that have not yet been revealed to you, but will be remembered by your Hearts and your Souls.

I, Shalamar, bless you with the Rose Red Ray of Love, Truth, Peace and Joy.

MASTERS, GUIDES
AND ANGELS

We, the Union of Love, and we, the Union of Light, we have sent you these Scriptions, for we know you are ready to receive them. We also know you are ready to release the doubt, the fear and the confusion. For understand, dear ones, your Joy is always within you, your Joy awaits you, your Joy longs for Union with your Soul, with your Body, and with your Mind. Your Joy waits patiently and silently deep within the Sacred Chamber of your Hearts. Your Joy's only journey is to express itself, to release itself into the world, into the Hearts of others, into the Earth, and into the Universe!

Joy is the Divine manifestation of Love, Joy is created from Love and Joy always returns back into the Heart of Love. For Love has many Dimensions, and Love expands beyond any horizon. Joy is Love's true expression of itself, Joy is pure and infinite, and there is nothing for you to do in order to feel Joy, other than to let go of doubt and fear and separation. Joy cannot be thought, Joy can only be felt, and only when Joy is felt, can the mind surrender to that feeling. Joy cannot be found in the mind, but the mind will accept Joy when it is felt.

We now need to share a very important Truth, a Truth that may not be understood to begin with, a Truth that may even sound silly, a Truth that may initially bring up a reaction of fear, of doubt, and of confusion. For understand, until you can realise we are all ONE, that we are all Love, your Joy may not find its way into full expression.

We, the Union of Love, and we, the Union of Light, are very aware of your concepts, and of your Spiritual journey to this moment. We understand your ideas of the Spiritual Realms, and we understand that you perceive many in the Spiritual Realms to be Masters, to be Guides, and to be Angels. This, of course, has served a Divine purpose to this moment, but now we wish to expand upon this concept that you have had for many thousands of Earth years.

We have already spoken that we believe and know that you are the Hueman Masters. We now need you to understand that you are also Hueman Guides for one another, and last but not least, that you are all Hueman Angels. And as we have already expressed in other Scriptions, you are all multifaceted, you are all Rainbows of magnificent and beautiful Light, and through your Divine Will, you have all physically manifested into your Earth Realm.

We need you now to understand the Mastership you possess in order to have made yourselves manifest in the Hueman form. We need you to realise the magnitude and the majesty of the Hueman form, as only true Masters, Guides and Angels could achieve such a Creation. And you, dear ones, are the physical living proof of this.

There are many Masters, Guides and Angels who also made themselves manifest on the earthly plane, and they were recognised to be so by other Hueman beings. The only difference between these Masters, Guides and Angels, and you, dear ones, is that they remembered who they were while experiencing their Hueman form. So you must now release yourselves from the idea that your Huemanity is some form of punishment, and is something that is less than what you call your Masters, your Guides and your Angels.

You must not see your incarnations as lessons or as hardship, for the true hardship, the only hardship, is that you have forgotten that you are Masters, Guides and Angels. You have perceived these Spiritual beings as something greater, something more, something to aspire to, and this, as we have explained to this point, has been Divine. However, understand you could not even perceive these Spiritual beings of greatness, of Love, and of sacrifice, unless these aspects were already within you. You cannot recognise something outside of you unless it is already within you, for as we have explained, everything is a reflection of everything else.

You all possess the minds of a Master, the gifts of a Guide, and the attributes of an Angel. It is time to take responsibility, to remember, to rejoice and reawaken to the Truth. You may wish to argue that if you are all these things, why is it so that there is so much cruelty, so much pain, so much disease, and so much conflict and confusion within so many Hueman beings. As we have expressed in other Scriptions, the journey of your Souls is to expand and to express, however, you have expanded and expressed so far from your Source, that you have forgotten who you truly are, and we are now here to remind you of the Truth of who you have always been.

Understand also the Souls, the Hueman beings that appear to have the most confusion, pain and struggle, are also the ones that have been brave enough to separate themselves completely from their Source, to experience and expand their own unique expression. An understanding of these Souls that are in such pain will not only be of assistance to them, but also to you.

So, for you to unlock the Joy in your Hearts, you must first release the fears, for many have become very attached to their fears, and when you are attached to your fears, you do not have to find the courage to release them. True courage can only come from a Soul willing to remember, a Soul that is 'sick and tired' of being sick and tired. And when the Soul finds courage to release the fears, the doubts, and the confusion of the mind, the Heart will open in gratitude, and bliss, and allow Joy to expand forth into every cell of you, the Hueman Master, of you, the Hueman Guide, and of you, the Hueman Angel.

So when we express this concept of jumping for Joy into the Abyss, into the Void, we are suggesting a moment of great wonder, of great Joy, so, do not fear your darkness, do not fear the Unknown, for when you truly step into the Sacred Void, your journey shall be lit with Joy.

THE MESSAGE OF METATRON

I, Metatron, I the Angel, I the Guide, I the Master, I am purely a reflection of you. I am no more or no less than you. The confirmation of who I am, I see in your Hearts and the confirmation of who you are, may be seen in my Heart. I, Metatron, I am what you may call an Archangel. I, too, am expanding, and expressing my Soul, my Light, my Joy, and I, as you, shall be brought back into Union, shall be brought back into the One Peace, the One Joy, and the One Heart.

As I speak, I speak for all Angelic Realms, for in service, we have separated ourselves from one another to bring you individual energies, individual expressions of the One Source. We have not minded the labelling, the descriptions, or even the misinformation of who we truly are. For we have served the purpose of being of service. However, now, like you, we wish to come back into Union with each other and our Source.

This does not mean we shall leave you, it does not mean that the Angelic Realms will end, however, it does mean greater Love and greater Light will be bestowed upon each Mind, Heart and Soul, for understand, many great things are happening within this Universe, and many new Realms are being created. It is not only you who are entering a New World. So are we, the Angels, for we are coming into Union with one another for the Grand Birth, for the next stage, if you choose, of evolution for this magnificent Universe.

Many new vibrations are being birthed, and what you call Masters and Guides are also coming into Union. They wish to move on, they wish to expand, they wish to embrace the Joy within, for when the Joy is birthed, much beauty is created, things beyond Hueman understanding are created, things even beyond our understanding are created.

For when you activate your Joy, you are allowing the Source within you and around you to also expand. You are giving the Mother and the Father a true gift, for they have only ever wished Joy for you, and when they experience your Joy, you experience theirs. So Union is taking place in many Realms, seen and unseen by you, and by us. Remember this Truth, for when you remember this Truth, you shall rejoice.

YOUR UNIVERSE
– A DIVINE
CONSCIOUSNESS

I, Shalamar, radiate Love and Peace to each of you. I, Shalamar, radiate Joy and Truth. I, Shalamar, speak for all the Union. I, Shalamar, now speak for your Universe, and all that resides within, for it is now time to understand that everything, be it a grain of sand, a grand canyon, a bird or a butterfly, all these things have a consciousness, and all these things are a part of the Divine Dance.

Everything plays a very important part in the whole, and to take this a step further, it is time for you to understand that every Star that shines, and every Planet that travels through this Universe, also has a consciousness.

Many of you are aware of this, and your Astrologers have served the Universe well, for they have given the Planets and Stars credibility, and have recognised their Divine design. However, as we have expressed to you, energetically, each Planet is related to your Diamond Light System, and we need you to understand, without a shadow of a doubt, that these Planets are also raising their consciousness, as you are raising yours.

Many new and wonderful energies are being birthed through these giants of Divine consciousness, and of course, as they expand, so do the many constellations of Cosmic Gateways that you call Star Systems. They, too, shall give birth to many new vibrational energies, and Scientists shall see proof of this sooner than they may realise, for not only do the Planets magnetically and spiritually have an effect on your entire being, but so do many of the Star constellations that surround your beautiful Planet Earth.

Of course, as you must understand, this knowledge would take an eternity to share, and even though we all have an eternity to explore, we must confine the knowledge to what is important at this point of your journey, or shall we say, for the next thousand of your years.

TEMPLE
OF THE MOON

MERCURY

MOON

EARTH

TEMPLE
OF THE MOON

I, Shalamar, wish to share with you this new knowledge, this wondrous time of expansion, and I shall begin with your Earth, which together with the Moon and Mercury, lies within the Sacred Triad of your Moon, where all the experiences of the Soul's evolution are made manifest through the physical being. And may we add, this includes all Soul vibrations whether they be Animal, Vegetable, Mineral or Ego.

THE EARTH

Your Earth, as you are realising, is a very Sacred Being indeed, and deserves your greatest respect and gratitude. However, you may not realise your Earth has sacrificed herself for the greatest expansion of the Hueman Soul. She has placed herself in a precarious position, but has done so of her own Divine Will.

She has waited for you to understand her, she has sent you many messages, mostly of Love, but some of despair. She, like her Brother and Sister Planets, has been given the Divine Call, if you choose, to expand herself and her consciousness. This is taking place, and will not be stopped.

New magnetic grids or what your ancient cultures often called "Songlines" are opening rapidly and being birthed. Many new Gateways within her Auric Field are being opened so they may receive the new vibrational medicine, if you choose, from the Planets and the Star Systems that surround her, for they are her neighbours and her family.

It is also time for you to realise that, since the beginning of your Earth's birth, there are many Inner Worlds that lie deep within her Heart and Soul. There are many Inner Kingdoms, of such beauty and such Light, that cannot be seen by the naked eye, but can be felt at a great depth within the Hueman Heart.

These Kingdoms now wish to come into Union with what we shall call the Outer Kingdoms of the Earth, where many Souls, whether they be Animal, Vegetable, Mineral or Hueman, reside. Many of you will begin to experience these Inner Kingdoms of the Earth, and we ask that you experience them with Love and Joy, and not in fear and separation, and through your intention to come into Union with these Inner Kingdoms, it shall be done.

So, just as you are awakening to your own Inner Kingdoms, and their Union, being that of your Heart and Soul, so the Earth is allowing her own Inner Kingdoms to come into Union, to be birthed, to be remembered, and to be received in Love and Joy.

So, understand, dear ones, when the Earth completes her Union of these Inner Kingdoms, your **Diamond Light of One** will also fully awaken, and you will experience an auric change, and a sense of its expansion, and a true glow will birth within your 'Shell of Light'.

As your Earth comes into Union with herself, so shall your 'Shell of Light' come into Union with hers, and great Joy and Light will fill the Sacred Shells of you and the Earth. Understand this may happen NOW. Again, it is only your willingness to choose such a Grand Union that is all that is required. Your Earth will guide each individual, if you listen with your Heart, and ask that your life rhythm, your Heart's beat, be brought into Union with the life rhythm of your Earth. For understand, it is the beat of your life rhythm that provides the music for your Divine Dance.

E
A
R
T
H

ONE DIAMOND LIGHT.

We wish now to bring forth into your Hueman consciousness an entity of great love and devotion, one that has been forgotten and denied within your perceptions. He is the Father of all Nature, and in Union with the Mother of All Nature, he is of service to her and her journey.

I, Lord Pan, bring myself before you in grace and gratitude. I, like my brother 'Fear', have often been misunderstood and conceptualised as some form of negativity. However, my love for Mother Nature and her beauty is my grandest destiny, and my greatest desire is to assist her in the fulfilment of her destiny.

I, the Father of All Nature, guard and protect her, and carry forth her Will with my actions. I am the Activator, if you choose, of all Mother Nature's cycles, and in Union we keep your World turning!

I am also the Gatekeeper of her Inner Kingdoms, and may I say, only with a pure Heart shall I allow you to proceed into them. Call me forth in your meditations and your reflections, as I wish to assist you with the Masculine aspect of your very Nature, for this, too, has been misunderstood and misaligned.

It is time, whether you be male or female in form, to find honour and reverence for the sexual nature of your beings, of which I am the Guardian. For your Society, and we, the Father and Mother of All Nature, cannot bear much more abuse and denial of this most sacred of energies.

I NOW SET BEFORE YOU MY

DEDICATION TO THE MOTHER

OF ALL NATURE, FOR THIS COMES

FROM MY HEART, IN GRATITUDE

FOR THE JOY OF OUR UNION.

I ALSO DEDICATE THIS TO YOU,

DEAR ONES, IN ANTICIPATION OF

THE JOY OF MY UNION WITH YOU,

FOR WITHIN EACH OF YOU

I, THE FATHER, AND SHE, THE

MOTHER OF YOUR NATURE, LIVE.

How I come to thee is with precious

abandonment of all consciousness.

For you are One with Darkness, precious Light,

and I forego all interpretation of your essence.

I see you beyond reach, and feel you beyond desire.

I ache in ecstasy for your touch,

and cry in Joy for my anticipation.

Trust does not exist in this plane of Light, for this plane

is the entrance to the majestic realisation of All Creation,

beyond doubt, and beyond thought.

Surrender, I, to the luscious embrace of rare Love

for all Love is rare to those who cannot surrender

to her whisper, and her wait.

I, Pan, seek you, dear Heart, and that place within

that no consciousness may conceive

for it is the Sacred House of Love, and all who enter

are rendered rich beyond Heaven and Earth.

I, Pan, guard the doorway of Love,

so too, Love has become my Guardian and my Guide.

LORD PAN – FATHER OF ALL NATURE

THE MOON

We move your consciousness now to the energy of your Moon, to the Pearl of your Solar System. Understand the magnetic magnitude of this Divine Being, for it is her energy that creates the ebb and flow of your great oceans, and as she is in Union with the waters of your world, she is also in Union with the Sacred waters of your bodies.

In her dedication to your Earth she allows the great cycles of Dark and Light to be made manifest upon her; to show Huemanity its own great inner cycles. And if you open your Heart to her, she will give you many gifts of Truth from other Realms, and other Dimensions, for she is a transformer of energy and she radiates Truth to those who wish to receive it. She does, however, protect the Truth with the Guardianship of Illusion.

The Moon has been perceived as the bringer of madness, of lunacy, of great confusion, however her Divine role is to radiate the Truth onto the darkened mind. She is the planet of purification, and the madness, or lunacy if you choose to call it this, is actually the process of purification of illusion within the mind. And trust us when we say her Light of Truth, her illumination of illusion is beginning to radiate and manifest at a much greater vibration.

She is a direct manifestation of the Dark and the Light, of the Feminine and the Masculine. However, she is also in Union with the left and right sides of your brain, and through your willingness, you may ask for the assistance of the Moon's pearlescent radiations to enhance and expand your psychic awareness.

You now need to open yourself to her Light, to her cycles, for she is one of the greatest tools for purification given to every form of consciousness on your planet. She will not deceive you, she will set you free, she will open you to the great cycles within every aspect of your being. For, as we have said previously, it is only when you resist your cycles that struggle and pain are created.

We do understand the dilemma of following your true and natural cycles, for you have created a world of great restrictions around yourselves. However, if you allow this Divine Light to work within your being, she will be gentle, she will be loving, and she will allow you to integrate, and transform yourselves at a gentle pace. For she, too, has been sent by the Divine, and no harm will come to those who fully embrace her, and the gift she wishes to give.

As you open to her Pearls of Wisdom, you will feel her deep within your body, in the **Diamond Light of Two**, opening you to the magic, the mystery, and the Love of many Dimensions. She will fill your being with Light, and your blood will carry her Truth, and when you carry her Truth, your physical being will vibrate with sheer Joy.

MOON

TWO DIAMOND LIGHT

43

Planets & Numbers Associated With Each Diamond Light

NEPTUNE & PLUTO	◆	10
URANUS	◆	9
SATURN	◆	8
JUPITER	◆	7
MARS	◆	6
SUN	◆	5
VENUS	◆	4
MERCURY	◆	3
MOON	◆	2
EARTH	◆	1

J
♥
Y

MERCURY

We now move gently toward the Divine Being you call Mercury; Mercury the messenger, Mercury the magnificent, and, as Mercury has been perceived as the Ruler of the Mind, it also now needs to be seen as a Bearer of New Thought.

It is, if you choose, in many ways, the Planet of the personality, of how you perceive yourselves for, as we have conveyed to you in other Scriptions, Mercury sits in the **Diamond Light of Three.** For this is where the Soul, when it enters through the Sacred Temple of your Hueman Being, this is where it begins to resonate with the Hueman condition of thinking, and the powerful vibration of thought within your Earthly Realm.

All Souls, on their Sacred Entrance to your Universe will, of course, pick up certain vibrational qualities from each Divine Planet. Many Souls that now enter are bringing new thoughts, new ways, and new will. As you may have been told many times, these beautiful babies, now entering your Dimension, are bringing with them new knowledge, and each of these Souls, when they come into Union with your Planet Mercury, will be receiving new thoughts and new personalities on their journey to the Earth Realm.

Mercury, being the Messenger, now brings tidings of great magnitude and importance. The message is that the Hueman mind is evolving quickly and precisely, and the Hueman mind will not be able to tolerate the illusions which have been created and programmed within it.

You will see among your younger generations, as you are now, an increase in what you think is confusion, illusion and mental disease and, as you look at these young Huemans, you may think they are confused, disturbed and scattered, however, many of them are actually releasing restrictive thought systems, inherited from their Ancestors, and are bringing new patterns of perception that older Hueman minds, still filled with illusion, cannot perceive. This, in itself, is a huge transition for all concerned, for all minds, no matter which part of the journey they find themselves experiencing.

Allow yourself to meditate on the Grand Messenger, allow its Love and its Truth of thought to permeate your mind, and allow this vibration of new thought and knowledge to come to rest in your **Diamond Light of Three**.

So, take time to understand your young ones, for they have the burden to integrate, assimilate, and then put into action these new thought forms. Listen to them, understand the great journey they have undertaken, and the great gift they are bringing to the Earth. For Illusion, as we have said, is the Guardian of Truth, and these brave young Souls now bring the Truth within their mental beings, and they need your support, not your resistance.

Allow Mercury to open you to give and receive divinely and, without hesitation, for the young one within you, and for the young of your Earth, as they have come to burst the bubbles of illusion, and may we suggest, to bring a new perception that will be of great service to all – but only if you choose to embrace it.

Your mind now needs to get past the idea of "outcomes", for this is the grandest illusion of all. Begin to see

MERCURY

THREE DIAMOND LIGHT

your life as an infinite, ever-changing journey of experiences, not a rigid dogma of beginnings and endings, that in between are filled with aimless, ego-driven goals. The traditional milestones that you have set up for yourselves are now being shattered by your youth, for they understand this new perception, and will not deny it. So, allow Mercury to re-awaken the purity of your own Inner Child, so you may inspire and honour all the children of your Earth, for blessed are the ones with eyes of innocence, for they shall see perfection and experience True Joy.

PLANETS & TEMPLES OF THE DIAMOND LIGHT SYSTEM

NEPTUNE & PLUTO — 10

TEMPLE OF THE STARS

URANUS — 9

SATURN — 8

JUPITER — 7

MARS — 6

TEMPLE OF THE SUN

SUN — 5

VENUS — 4

MERCURY — 3

MOON — 2

TEMPLE OF THE MOON

EARTH — 1

JOY

I, Shalamar, would like, in conclusion, to bring to these Divine Beings of your Earth, your Moon and your Mercury, a very powerful concept, so that your Union with these Planets of Grand Consciousness will be made beautifully, eloquently, but most of all, simply. Understand that this Sacred Triad of your Moon represents your Soul's experience of Union with your Hueman bodies.

We suggest that you perceive these Planetary Beings, that lay within you and around you in your Universe, as correlating and initiating the many levels of your own Divine Being. Hence, understand, your Earth is a reflection of your physical being, and when you come into Union with your planet Earth, you will bring much support and a great wealth of health to your physical body.

Your Moon, which governs the great oceans of your world, is also a direct reflection of your Hueman emotions, and when you come into Union with your glorious Moon, you will come into Union with your emotional being, the being through which we communicate with feeling.

Understand that your Mercury, even though it is positioned in the Sacred Triad of your Moon, does as we have explained, govern aspects of your Hueman mind, and when you come into Union with your Mercury, you will come to understand the depth and the beauty of the Hueman mind. You will come into Union with its uniqueness and its Eternal Source of Creativity.

So, within your Hueman Realm, the Realm in which you express your Huemanness, your physical Hueman experience is governed by, and is in direct Union with your Earth, your emotional Hueman experience is governed by, and is in direct Union with your Moon, and your mental Hueman experience is governed by, and is in direct Union with your Mercury. When these are all balanced, and in harmony, so shall all your Hueman experiences become a grand Joy indeed.

TEMPLE OF THE SUN

MARS

SUN

VENUS

TEMPLE OF THE SUN

I, Shalamar, now move into the Sacred Triad of your Sun,
where all the experiences of your Soul's evolution are expressed
through your Heart. Understand, that in these teachings, the
Planets of your Universe have been carefully placed, and as
these Scriptions unfold, so the understanding of why they have
been brought into Union with certain Diamond Lights
will become crystal clear.

We shall begin with your Venus which, through the ages,
you have called your Planet of Love, and your Planet of the
Arts. We wish to express to you now why this magnificent
being was given such an identity.

VENUS

When your Soul enters this Universe, and travels through the Cosmic Tree of life, it receives certain vibrations which become part of the Soul's journey, in preparation for its arrival into physical manifestation upon the Earth plane.

Your Planet Venus is a Grand Gateway indeed, and for the purpose of the teaching, we wish to initiate you into a Truth, for as you know, Venus sits within the Sacred Gateway of your Soul, where your Soul has come to express itself, through the Diamond Light of Four.

As your Soul, in all its incarnations, travels through the Divine Consciousness of these Grand Planetary Beings, it arrives in the Sacred Realm of Venus and this is where, for the purpose and expansion of Love within this **Diamond Light of Four**, it comes into Union with other Souls with whom it has chosen to share a Hueman experience.

On your journey to your Earth plane, even if some of the Souls you are to be in Union with, have already manifested on the physical level, you will still be in Union with them in the Sacred Realm of Venus. As in Scriptions expressed by Father Time, your Heart and your Soul are not constrained by time or space.

Often your Soul will journey to Venus, to come into Union with the other Souls that are already manifest, or are becoming manifest on Earth. It is a place of Grand Union for Souls that wish to integrate and communicate about the path ahead. It is a place of great beauty and great Truth.

In your own meditations, we ask that you consciously journey there, for it is a place of nourishment and enlightenment for your Soul's expansion. It is a Realm of great Love and remembrance of why you have chosen Union with certain Souls whilst on your Earth walk. It is where you may go to commune with other Souls that you may be in conflict with, during your Earth experience. It is where you can reach resolution, and where you can remember the Love, and the Truth of how you are to be of service to other Souls. It is where the Soul may also rest during your meditation and dream states. It is where the Soul can remember those aspects of the physical journey it has chosen for itself, and why.

We wish for you now to remember this: In your dark nights, in your loneliness, your Venus shines brightly above, as the Morning and Evening Star. It never leaves you, and it burns brightly to remind you that in service, it soothes, nourishes, and re-awakens your Soul to its path.

Venus has also been called the Goddess of Love, and it represents the Love and tenderness of the Mother, for understand, each Soul is the most precious of children to the Mother. Re-awaken your remembrance of this Planet of Love, and enter its Holy Realm so you may be guided and supported in all your relationships upon the Earth plane and beyond.

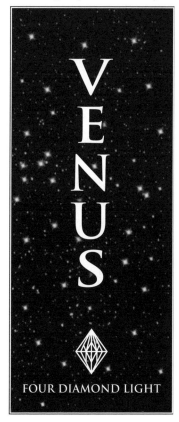

VENUS

FOUR DIAMOND LIGHT

THE SUN

We now come to the Grand Being of your Sun, and we find it difficult to relate to you what this Being of such Grand Light truly is, for, as we have expressed in other Scriptions, it is an energy beyond words, it is a Diamond Light beyond our expression. So, bear with us as we try to convey what you need to know.

Your Sun, we would like to say, is the Grandest Gateway of all that has been made into physical manifestation for your Hueman experience. It is not that it is grand, so much in its vibration, for all the Planets are pure and Divine, it is grand, however, in what can be accessed and made manifest when true Union with this Being, you call the Sun, is activated. For, it is not only the Life-Force of your Hueman world, it is also the Life-Force for all in your Solar System, seen and unseen by you.

We know that other Planets have other Suns and other Moons, however, this Sun, for the purpose of the teaching, must now be seen as the physical manifestation of Source, of the Grand Creator, of the Great Grand Father of this Universe. It is, in Truth, of both the Feminine and Masculine energies, but we wish, for the purpose and ease of your Hueman mind, or shall we say your Mercurial mind, that you perceive it as a Masculine aspect, which has been so in many teachings to this point.

It is the Gateway through which energies from other Universes may enter. It allows other Realms, as yet not understood by you, to receive as they enter, the Essence of your Universe, or shall we say, the Essential Sensory Perception of your Universe.

Your Sun, which resides, as we have said, within your own Hearts, and within the **Diamond Light of your Five**, now needs to be perceived as the Sacred Flame of the Divine Source, for this, in Truth, is what it is. It is the Life-Force of the Divine made manifest. Within this Sun are many Dimensions and many Realms, however, for the purpose of these Scriptions, we wish to tell you of Four Realms that lay deep within the Heart of your Sun and your Hueman bodies; Four Sacred Chambers that may be accessed by you at this time of your evolution.

There are many ways to perceive these Chambers, and this is where our difficulty begins, for understand, the knowledge that we impart now is only a small aspect of a grander vision. We know, however, that when you hear these words with your Heart, it will allow you to experience and expand upon what cannot be spoken in Hueman words.

The First Sacred Chamber within this, the Divine Flame, is one that will connect you to all civilizations that have been made manifest within your Earth Realm, dating back to your most ancient Brothers and Sisters. This is where all knowledge, but more importantly, where the Pure Essence of your Ancients, may be received and remembered within your own Hearts. It is a Chamber of Grand Remembrance of all who have gone before you, and will also allow you to recall your own past lives within these Civilizations.

The Second Sacred Chamber, we wish to introduce you to, is the Chamber of your Spiritual Guidance. It is the Chamber where all aspects of those which you have perceived as Masters, Guides and Angels may be accessed, and where you can receive the highest guidance and support for the journey of your Soul. It is a grand aspect indeed, and may be entered into with your pure willingness to receive, and to remember you are not alone on your Soul's journey.

The Third Sacred Chamber within this Divine Being, your Sun, is the Chamber of your Ancestors, where all your genetic coding, and your unique cellular make-up may be accessed, rejuvenated, and even healed. It is where you may come into Union with your Ancestors, whether they be of this Universe, or Beyond.

This Third Sacred Chamber is a place of cellular regeneration, and it will serve you well, for it will support and accelerate your cellular being back into the Light Body from which it originated, and it will become an important part of your Spiritual routine, your Spiritual growth, and your Soul's expansion.

The Fourth Sacred Chamber is one of pure Light. It is one of pure Love, and it is where the Heart may return to remember its very essence. It is where the Heart may return to come into Union with the Heart of God and Goddess. It is the Sacred Chamber of true Union while in the Hueman experience. It is the Chamber of the Heart's Fire, the Heart's Truth, and the Heart's Joy. It is where you may instantaneously come into Union with the Divine Heart of Pure Source.

As we speak of these Four Chambers, we wish to bring your remembrance to the Infinite Braids of Light, these Four aspects of Eternal Memory, Eternal Motion, the Male/Fire aspect and the Female/Water aspect. These Infinite Braids of Light, these Four aspects, are one and the same as these Four Sacred Chambers within your Sacred Central Sun.

The First Chamber is your 'Eternal Motion', the Chamber of all civilizations that you have walked through, and experienced.

The Second Chamber is your 'Eternal Memory', your Highest Consciousness reconnecting with your unseen Spiritual brethren and family, your true family, your family of Light, and those which, to this point, you have called your Masters, Guides and Angels. However, we ask you to remember that eternally, you are all One!

The Third Chamber of your Divine Being is what you may relate to as your Feminine/Water aspect. For, understand, you are predominately water, and your cellular memory and your energy cannot exist without the gift of water. This Feminine aspect, as we have said, also represents the Waterfall Way; the grand journey of your Soul through your Ancestors, and through your cells.

And, of course, the Fourth Chamber relates to your Male/Fire aspect, the Life-Force of the Divine Flame that burns deep within your Heart.

These Four Sacred Chambers, of which we speak, that lie within your Central Sun, are also the same Braids of Sacred Light that make your Hueman journey Sacred. Understand that it is only through your Divine Will that you may enter all these Chambers, however, we do suggest that you always begin your Union in the Sacred Chamber of One, whether you choose to complete all Four Chambers, or less, in a meditation state of being. For each one of these Chambers is extremely powerful, and there is a method in our madness when we ask you to always begin in the Chamber of One, and proceed to the Chamber of Two, then Three, and finally, Four.

Understand that, as an Initiate of the Heart, you, through your own intention, may experience many different levels within these Sacred Chambers, so that your Joy may travel through your Infinite Braids of Light, and be made manifest beyond your Hueman imagination.

THE INFINITE BRAIDS OF LIGHT

ETERNAL MEMORY

MALE/FIRE
ASPECT

FEMALE/WATER
ASPECT

ETERNAL MOTION

JOY

SACRED CHAMBERS OF THE SUN

2
SPIRITUAL
GUIDANCE

4
TRUE
UNION

3
YOUR
ANCESTORS

1
GRAND
REMEMBRANCE

J
♥
Y

MARS

I, Shalamar, draw your attention to what has been perceived, to this point, as another fiery Being, your planet Mars. It has often been perceived as a Planet of War, as Masculine in nature, and as a Planet of assertion and action. Up to this point, it has been true, but Mars now wishes to transform this perception to become more of who it truly is, which is actually not a Planet of War but a Planet of the Warrior.

In its essence, Mars is the Spiritual Warrior, and a Spiritual Warrior works with the intention of peace, and moves through time and space as a loving peaceful energy. The Spiritual Warrior carries the Truth that executes Divine Will. It upholds that Truth, protects peace, and refuses conflict. As we have expressed, the House of your Free Will and your Divine Will rest within the region of your **Diamond Light of Six**, and as in previous Scriptions, when Union of the Sun and Mars is made manifest, then the Divine Will may work through the Heart.

The Spiritual Warrior stands for the Will of the Divine, the Will of Love, and the determination of peace, for peace shall not budge from its position as the foundation for passion, and we wish to expand upon the necessity for passion to be expressed from the foundation of peace. If the foundation of peace is not present, passion cannot be harnessed, cannot be made manifest into Truth, and its highest purpose.

Passion, without the foundation of peace, can quickly transform into the energy of lust, passion can transform into the energy of anger, and passion without peace can transform into the energy of violence. For understand, war, conflict, and lust have been birthed from passion that has not had the foundation of inner peace to support it.

So, your perceptions of what you call the God of War must now change, for Mars must be seen as the Spiritual Warrior who walks in peace with the passion of its purpose. And when you can embrace and re-awaken the Spiritual Warrior within you, you shall find peace, and you shall have Eternal Truth, and once more Joy shall be brought forth in all your actions. As I, Shalamar, now bring to conclusion the Sacred Triad of your Sun, understand that this Sacred Triad of your Sun represents your Soul's experience of Union with your Heart.

Venus reflects the Love relationships of your Soul whilst on the Earthly plane. The Sun reflects the Soul's expression of that Love whilst on the Earthly plane, and Mars reflects the Highest Will of your Soul and its true purpose. So, when you come into conscious Union with your Venus, you will come into conscious Soul Union with all your relationships while in the Hueman experience.

As you come into Union with your Sun, you will come into Union with your Soul's experiences of Love, whether they be in this Earthly Realm, or beyond.

When you come into Union with your Mars, you will come into Union with the Will of your Soul, and with your Soul's remembrance of its Divinity, and its true purpose as a Spiritual Warrior.

So, as the Temple of your Moon represents your Soul's physical experience, the Temple of your Sun represents your Soul's Heart experience, and I, Shalamar, shall now ascend you to the Temple of your Stars, which represents your Soul's mental experience and knowledge.

MARS

SIX DIAMOND LIGHT

TEMPLE
OF THE STARS

URANUS

SATURN

JUPITER

TEMPLE OF THE STARS

I, Shalamar, give you the Rose Red Ray of remembrance,

the Rose Red Ray of your return to the Heart of your Source.

I, Shalamar, have gratitude for the challenges you present to us,

and await conscious Union with you, the multi-faceted, multi-

dimensional Beings of Light that you are, and are Becoming.

This third Holy Triad of your Stars is such a

grand vision, is such a subject of great beauty and Infinite

Knowledge, and is where the Higher Consciousness of the

Soul may be remembered. Understand, we do not intentionally

hold any Truth back from you, dear ones, however we do, with

intention, design these Scriptions so they may be accepted

firstly by your Minds, and secondly, easily remembered

by your Hearts and your Souls.

JUPITER

We begin with a Grand Being, a Being that has been known as one of expansion, of growth, and even of opportunity, and what you call 'Luck', and may I add that the idea of what you call 'Luck' is one of your grandest illusions of all. For, understand, illusion can be found in all polarities, all aspects, including those which you perceive as positive.

Your mind tells you luck is something you require, usually when you are 'stuck'; when you cannot find the courage to enter into your Hearts and your Souls, to find your way, to find your true path. Luck is what you may call your good karma, so luck in your perception is like a lottery, luck appears as a mysterious gift. Many will say to another, "Aren't you lucky to have what you have" or "didn't you have a lucky escape".

You also hold the notion within your consciousness that there is also 'bad luck', and that through no fault of your own, through no responsible action, or inaction on your part, you believe you can receive 'good' or 'bad luck'. All is pre-destined, dear ones, this is something you must understand now, however, what you may not easily understand is that you are the ones who plotted, planned, and mapped your own destinies, for the Soul purpose of your expansion, your growth, and your experience.

You wonder at your clairvoyants, prophets and soothsayers, and you may be in awe of their gifts when they tell you of your past, your present and your future. Understand, even if these intuitive ones do not know it themselves, what they are actually doing is tapping into what we would like to call your Life Books.

In Union with certain other Souls, no matter of which Vibration or

Realm, you write you own Life Book. You design your own pain and sorrow, your own fortune and misfortune, for understand, whether your experiences appear to your Hueman consciousness as good or bad, they have all been created with your Divine Wills, *always for the experience and expansion of Love.*

When you can really understand this concept of Truth, then you will begin to harness and embrace your life, and its ultimate path of Joy. When you can take responsibility, and understand that before you even came to your Earth Realm, you had planned all your experiences, only then can you release the many limiting aspects of yourself, and only then can you understand them, and the Divine parts they have had to play in your Earth walk.

So, as we bring your attention now to your Planet Jupiter, the Planet of expansion and growth, the Planet of your so called 'luck', for whereas it sits in the **Diamond Light of your Seven**, of your mind, of your Spiritual sight, know that it is also where you may access the opportunities and the challenges that you have given yourself. It is also where you can detach from the emotion, and the outcome of such challenges and opportunities, and see the grander vision of what they represent in your growth and your expansion.

Jupiter, in its very size (mass) is symbolically of great importance, for within this Universe in which you dwell, one of your greatest gifts and challenges is that of your mind; of how you perceive your world through your Spiritual vision, or shall we say, your lack of it.

SEVEN DIAMOND LIGHT

Jupiter radiates grand vision, Jupiter emanates the Christ Consciousness. Again, it is your choice, with the action of your own Divine Will, that through this Divine Being of Jupiter you may access the Highest of Consciousness available within your Universe.

Jupiter may be meditated upon to activate your Spiritual Sight, to allow you to see within yourself; to journey through that Inner Eye into the physical, mental and emotional beings that lay deep within, and around, your body.

Also understand that, with the grand power and vision of such a Planet, there must also be the balance of initiation, if you choose, before you may come into complete Union with these powerful energies. For Jupiter, as we begin to show you, is also where your greatest fears may be manifest. As it is the Planet of expansion, and growth, even wealth, the negative aspects of such a Being are greed and great self-doubt.

So we bring your consciousness back once more into the Realm of that Divine being you call Fear, for as we have expressed, Fear has been your greatest friend. And we would like to share with you another Truth, a grand and very important Truth for all Souls in their experience of expansion and remembrance, for until you can completely understand that which we are about to express, your journey will continue to be one of struggle, and not one of Joy.

Fear, dear ones, Fear is the Guardian to the Gateways of your Ascension. Fear stands strong and brave at each of the Gateways that we shall call Divine Beings, these Planets of your Universe. Within each of these Beings is a Gateway, a plane of ascension back into the purity, back into the remembrance of your true essence. Each and every Divine Being in your Universe is guarded by Fear, and this includes you, however the Planet Jupiter, shall we say, has one of the grandest Gatekeepers of all, and that is the Fear of Lack.

Shall we say it another way: when you fear Lack, you think you require Luck, and when you think you require Luck, there is no trust or faith in the Heart and Soul that with Love has plotted and planned, in every detail, your present life path.

So, dear ones, bathe in the expansion of Love and Light which your Grand Jupiter has to offer, walk through the Gateway of Fear, through the illusion of your mind and your frightened ego. Allow yourself to detach and remember that every experience, every situation, is an opportunity of abundance, whether it be an abundance of material wealth, an abundance of health, an abundance of Love or an abundance of knowledge through experience.

Allow Jupiter to evaporate your illusion of Lack, whether it be Lack of Love, Lack of Light, Lack of Joy or even, with great sadness, we say Lack of Deserving. For to fear that you do not deserve means you *de-serve* yourself. It means you are opposing the gift of giving to yourself, the gift of service to yourself. Remember, dear ones, a very important equation:

The VISION you hold of yourself, in Union with the SERVICE of your Soul, fuelled by the PASSION in your Heart is the KEY to your highest path of JOY.

Understand, dear ones, that your passion and its intensity is created from the expansion of your Soul's desire, and know this: your Soul's skills will always match your Soul's desires. This is Universal Law. Trust your Soul's desire, fill it with Love and strengthen it with trust. There is nothing too great, no vision too broad, that cannot be conceived and created by all of you.

SATURN

I, Shalamar, now bring to you with the greatest reverance and respect, the grace and the beauty of your Planet Saturn. This is a Being of great gifts, and magnificent Light, and irrespective of whether you see it as a positive or negative assertion, only a very small part of Saturn's essence has been made known to your Hueman consciousness.

Saturn, rightfully so, has been perceived as Father Time, and as in previous Scriptions, much of Saturn's energy, known to this point, may be perceived and received in the message of Father Time.

The knowledge that Father Time is now leaving the Divine Consciousness of your Planet Earth has been shared with you, and this brings you to a grand and wonderful discovery indeed, the discovery of what else lies deep within the Heart of that which you have called your Grand Teacher, your Father of Time, and your Planet of restrictions and limitations. For, when the true essence of Saturn is revealed and understood by you, you will wish to change even the interpretations of your astrological charts.

Saturn, in your understanding, has a cycle of twenty-nine years for one revolution in your Solar System, and as we take these numerical symbols of the Two and the Nine, we discover that within the Diamond Light of Two is the foundation, or the base of your physical being, and within the Diamond Light of Nine is what we call the highest aspect of your Soul, your Soul Star.

Understand that the Two and the Nine create the number Eleven, and as we have explained to you in past Scriptions, Eleven is the number of your Elohim, of your equality with God/Goddess/All That Is. So, with everything *within*, and *not within* your Universe, the language of symbology, and the language of numerals, can deliver many Truths.

Saturn's twenty-nine year cycle is no accident, for it represents your Eleven, but more than that, it is the flashpoint of Union it is the Divine Birth of your Soul (the Nine Diamond Light) coming into creation, and into Union with your Hueman being (your Two Diamond Light). As it has been explained to you, the **Eight Diamond Light**, that of your Planet Saturn, is also the symbol of Infinity, of your Waterfall Way, the journey of your Soul.

Your Saturn is where your Soul comes into being in the physical Earth Realm. It is the Birth Canal, if you choose, of your Soul into physical form, and for the purpose of these teachings, as much as your Saturn has been perceived as Masculine in its essence, we wish now to expand your consciousness into the Femininity of such a Divine Being, the Love of such a Divine Being, and the grace and the beauty that lay deep within the Heart of Saturn.

Saturn has certainly radiated many limitations, it has radiated many teachings through the lessons of restriction, and as we have expressed in previous Scriptions, it is a Grand Soul indeed that wishes to contain itself within the limitations of a Hueman body. It is the path of the Master, the Angel and the Guide, that a Grand Soul, through its own Divine Will, chooses such a limiting experience, with the greatest creation of limitation within your Universe being your perception of Time.

SATURN

EIGHT DIAMOND LIGHT

We wish to take this essence of Time and *reverse* it, reverse it now, so that it may *emit* the remembrance of the true Heart of your Saturn, so it may *emit* radiations of the Courage, the Will, and the Passion that is required to be birthed into such limiting conditions. For this is the gift that Saturn, the Feminine aspect, the Universal Mother, now wishes you to remember, and to embrace. For when you remember your courage, your will, and the grace with which you have birthed yourself, this shall be the Truth of your worth, of your Divinity, and of your entitlement to receive the gift of remembering the true nature of your journey.

Father Time now wishes to release itself, so the Mother may radiate into your Heart and Soul, the remembrance of your own grace, courage and beauty; that you may remember, not the restrictions and limitations in which you find yourself, but to rejoice in the courage, and the Divine Will of your very essence.

Allow the figure of **Eight**, within this **Diamond Light of Saturn**, to dance and move and flow and rejoice in this Truth, and when you allow this, your entire physical being will be open to the grace and the beauty within. So, do not permit the illusion of Time to restrict you and hold you within its limits. Allow your Heart and your Soul to joyously emanate the radiance of their essence, and their freedom.

URANUS

I, Shalamar, now welcome you to a most auspicious and Grand Being of cosmic consciousness, a treasure of remembrance, a Universal Lightbearer of Grand Knowledge. Uranus is a quiet achiever, Uranus is a Being that does not look for recognition. It is the first Grand Gatekeeper, if you choose, the first stop for any Soul coming into this Universe. It holds within it such grand vision, such overwhelming power of Life, and its Force. To open your Heart and your Higher Mind to what is within its Realms, will open you to All Knowledge within this, your Universe.

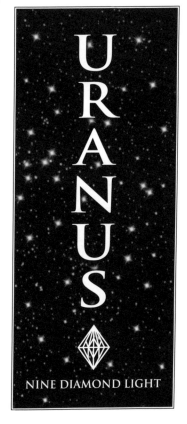

Every Soul, seen and unseen by you, before you, with you, or beyond you, will have grand memories of its Union with this Planet you call Uranus. It is where you may access what you have called your Akashic Records; it is where you may access all experiences of your past and your future. As we have explained and expressed in other Scriptions, your Uranus, your **Ninth Diamond Light**, represents the manifestations of your very Souls, and the journeys within this, your Universe.

NINE DIAMOND LIGHT

It is where the Spirit, if you choose, is magnetized into its chosen expression, and its future attraction of experience and expansion. It is a Cosmic Gateway through which the Soul may remember its very first experience of this Universe.

The beauty, the Light and the Love of this Grand Master is hard to put into terms of description. It is where the beginning of your Time and its events may be found, and it is where the end of your Time and its events may be discovered.

As we have expressed to you in our Scriptions the presence of other Star Nations, who have come to be of assistance to your Earth Realm, we now wish to introduce to you the Uranian Race that resides within this magnificent Being of Cosmic Consciousness. For, understand, each of your Planets has, within it, a Civilisation, and future Scriptions will invite you to come into Union with them. However, for the purpose of these teachings, and the understanding of your very Souls, we wish you to know that the Civilisation of the Uranians is one of great importance for the evolution of your Universe, of your Souls, and of your own Civilisation.

Each of you has, what we wish to express as, a Uranian Guide. This Uranian Guide is a guardian of your very Soul, and is a nourisher, nurturer, and counsel of your Soul, while it is in expression, within this, your Solar System and Universe.

Please do not confuse this with your Masters, Guides and Angels, for they too are present within this Universe, but may we say, they also have many expressions in other Universes, and other Realms. They are also guardians, nourishers, nurturers and counsellors of your Spirit, of your Soul, and of your physical being, whether it be in this Universe or Beyond. However, the Uranian Guide's specific tasks, their services to you are as the coach, if you choose, the inspirer, the watcher, the witness of your Soul's unique experience while in an Earthly expression.

They have chosen, to this point, not to commune with many at all, not even to express their existence. However, as Uranus in these teachings will now represent the Spiritual Intellect, the intuitive aspect of your Higher Minds, they now wish to invite themselves into your Highest Consciousness, so they may work intimately and Divinely with the journeys of your Souls. You are ready, dear ones, for such Truth and such Knowledge, and to be frank, without the Truth and Knowledge now wishing to be expressed to you, your experience and your expansion as a Soul will not be adequate, or even nourishing.

Understand also, when you come into Union with your Soul's Uranian Guide, from that Union, your connections to Civilisations within the other Planets can be made with ease, with grace, and with Joy.

We suggest that in your peaceful space, in your joyous space, in your space of silence, that you become aware, and connect with your **Diamond Light of Nine**, the Highest aspect of your Consciousness. Ask, through your desire and intention, that you may come into Union and communion with your Uranian Soul Guide, and when Union has taken place, and communion has begun, your Soul shall experience peace and Joy and expansion. It shall receive nourishment, nurturing, and an infinite flow of Life-Force, of God-Spark within its very Being.

Much will be discovered about this Grand Consciousness of Uranus that has not been revealed until this time. It is truly a grand awakener of vision, and of remembrance of the very beginning of your Universe. It has always emanated a frequency that your Soul resonates with and is nourished by, however, this has been, to this point, an unconscious Union. As with all Union, and all communion, the *conscious* awareness of this within your Hueman experience is the very key, the very quickener, that allows true expansions on all levels, within all Realms of your own being and beyond.

I, Shalamar, am grateful for the Divine Will of Uranus to come forth and to share its gifts of service. Show this Divine Being your gratitude for its gifts, and it shall show you the grandest visions of Truth and Universal Knowledge.

So, understand now, dear ones, that the Sacred Triad of your Stars represents the experience of your Spiritual or Divine Consciousness, while in the Hueman experience.

Jupiter is the physical manifestation of the Higher Mind, creating visions within the Hueman experience that are emanated from the Third Eye.

Saturn reflects the emotional experience of the Spirit, hence the Mother returning to embrace you through her thought and vision.

Uranus represents the highest intelligence of the Spirit, and remembrance of the Spirit's experience, through the vehicle of its Hueman Soul.

NEPTUNE AND PLUTO

This Tenth Diamond Light, as already expressed, holds within it the energies of Neptune and Pluto, and for the purpose of the teachings, we wish to express them in a way that the Mind may understand, the Heart may experience, and the Soul may remember.

The **Tenth Diamond Light** is the Gateway to Goddess and God, to the Unmanifest and Creation, and these two Grand Beings of Neptune and Pluto, in their vibrations represent the Feminine and Masculine aspects of All Source. They are the Guardians of what you may perceive as Heaven itself.

Understand that everything in your Universe has within it the Feminine and Masculine Forces of Life, however, for the purpose of these Scriptions, we wish to highlight the dominant aspects within these Grand Beings.

Your Planet Neptune is, in essence, Feminine by nature, and within her may be found great depths of intuition and illumination. We ask that you perceive Neptune as the Gatekeeper of the Goddess, as from the Sacred Waters of the Mother, all Souls are birthed, and carried forth on their journey.

Pluto, by its very nature, is the spark-lighter and initiator for all Souls. He is the mover and the shaker of your consciousness and, in essence, he is the Sacred Fire of your Spirit. Being the Masculine aspect, we ask that you perceive Pluto as the Gatekeeper of the God, of the Divine Heart.

By coming into conscious Union with your Neptune and your Pluto, you will begin to understand your true Spiritual Mother and Father, for they represent, and are also the physical manifestations of, the Grand Mother and the Grand Father that radiate beyond your Universe.

For it is the Grand Mother and the Grand Father that embrace your Spirit, your Soul and your Divine Essence. And it is they that place you in the arms of the Guardians Neptune and Pluto, so that the vehicle of your Spirit, your Soul, may be re-awakened and placed within the Waterfall Way for your journey of expansion, until you return back into your own Spirit, and the Spirit of the Grand Mother and the Grand Father.

These Divine Beings, Neptune and Pluto, wish to serve you in the remembrance of your true essence, and awaken your consciousness to this Universe and Beyond, where you may begin to remember and rejoice in the very majesty and magnificence of your true Spirit. For, understand, this Universe is not your Home -

YOUR SPIRIT IS YOUR HOME

I, Shalamar, have been sent to you through the Union of Love and Light, through the Union of the Grand Mother and the Grand Father, and it is my greatest Joy to be of service to each and every Soul that is willing to remember its Spirit, its Home. For each Home is filled with Joy; each Home is filled with Love and Light; each Home is a Divine Spirit made manifest into the Fire and the Water of the Grand Father and the Grand Mother.

With the grandest vision I have for each of you, I, Shalamar, walk beside you in Joy and remembrance of who each of you truly are.

NEPTUNE & PLUTO

TEN DIAMOND LIGHT.

THE GRAND CYCLE
OF SERVICE

We, the Union of Love and the Union of Light, reflect to you our very design, for understand, your design is our design, and all design is the Divine Signature of the One. Your consciousness is an aspect of our consciousness, and our consciousness is an aspect of yours. Every design is interrelated, interconnected, and in Truth is One. However, through individual expression, through individual experience, and through individual Soul essence, it is easy to forget the Oneness of All That Is.

We have expressed to you that you, as a Huemanity, can also be called a Group Consciousness. This, of course, is Truth, however we wish to expand the expression of your Group Consciousness, and for you to be open to receive the very Truth of your unique Hueman expressions.

Understand that your Solar System is also a Group Consciousness of its own design, and we wish you now to perceive, if you can, that we, the Union of Love, and we, the Union of Light, are the Guardians of several Group Souls, and of several Grand Consciousnesses.

We are the Guardians of the Grand Consciousness of your Universe, of your Solar System, of your Huemanity, and of your very experience. And we watch in awe and wonder as we observe, with such grand vision, all of these unique expressions within this, your Universe, now returning back into one Grand Light of Love. So, as you are a unique expression of your Huemanity, each of the Planets is a unique expression of their Solar System, and last but definitely not least, your Universe is a unique expression of the Group Consciousness of All

Universes. What is beyond that we cannot say, for no words exist.

We have expressed to you in other Scriptions that your Solar System and your Universe are, like you, experiencing magnificent growth and expansion. The Cosmic Dance, if you choose, that is within you and around you, is about to learn some new dance steps. It is about to find itself hearing a new tune, dancing a new dance, expressing a new Joy.

As we guard your Universe, we wait to show you other magnificent Universes of such beauty, such uniqueness, and these will be given great detail in future Scriptions. But for this *now* moment of Eternal Timelessness, we shall remain within the Realm of this your Universe, of this your Solar System, of this your Huemanity, and of this your unique Hueman experience.

With regard to your Hueman experience, we wish to share with you another Truth, for understand, all things within your Universe have a Heart and a Soul for their own creation, and have experiences through their own Will. You, dear ones, you also, in Hueman expression, have your Heart and Soul, have your expressions of experience, but in addition you also have the gift of *MOVEMENT* and of *FREEDOM*.

As we have expressed, our design is your design, and our design, like yours, is the design of freedom, of change, of movement, and in that freedom, change, and movement, this allows you to experience all things, and within you, all things exist.

You are of the Earth, you are of all the Planets in the Solar System, you are of the Stars around these Planets, you are of this Universe, but more importantly, you are of all things outside your Universe. You are of all things beyond your Hueman mind's perception; you are of all things beyond your Soul's perception and conception; and you are of all things within the Heart of your essence, and more.

Understand that the power, the purpose, and even the passion of your Planets, of your Stars, and of your Universe are grand attributes indeed, however their consciousness does not allow them the *freedom* of *movement* and *change* that has been gifted to you, dear ones. They have been fixed to a point within their design, for the purposes of the beings that reside within and around them.

You, dear ones, if you care to remember, if you have the courage to remember, you will know that you are not a Group Consciousness just of Huemanity, but a Group Consciousness of Masters, of Angels and of Spiritual Guides, and that the Grand Mother and the Grand Father of All That Is allows you to create and co-exist within this place you call your Earth, your Solar System and your Universe.

You may perceive yourselves to be whatever you wish to be at any one moment and, through the gift of your imagination, you may experience all levels of emotion and thought. We ask you now to perceive this:-

A UNIVERSE THAT HAS BEEN CREATED SOLELY TO BE OF SERVICE TO YOU, THROUGH THE DIVINE WILL AND CONSCIOUSNESS OF ITS GRAND BEINGS, THE PLANETS AND THE STARS.

When you remember and embrace this Grand Truth, your very Heart will explode into ecstasy, and you will remember your purity and your innocence. You will be overwhelmed with humility and gratitude for such grand gifts as your Earth, your Solar System, and your Universe. And when you realise the service and selflessness of the Love being expressed to you through these Grand Beings of Planets, Stars and the Universe, you may begin to understand and to nurture all aspects of yourself, and the Universe in which you find yourself.

Understand, this Grand Cycle of Service that has been gifted to you is now completing itself. The Universe, and all within it, is now expanding for their experience and their growth.

It will be your gratitude for the gifts of expansion and reflection, that this Universe has given you, that will create the very Gateway that allows Union to take place between this Universe, and other magnificent Universes, Solar Systems, and Master Races. It will be your gratitude, and your willingness to be of service now, that will allow everything in your Universe to expand, to experience, and to embrace its own Joy, its own Light, and its own Divine Path back into the One Heart.

You, dear ones, are all Divine Channels. The radiations, the very essence of the Planets of your Solar System, you channel through your Beings, and through your Diamond Light Systems. You also channel each other's Pain, Fear, Love and Joy. You channel the essence of the Earth and, in your Union with each other, you channel the very Life-Force of Creation itself. Each of your Diamond Lights is a Sacred Gateway through which you may channel to another. Each of these Diamond Lights is a Sacred Gateway for you to channel your desire, and willingness to be in Union with everything in your Universe.

Your Diamond Light Systems, dear ones, do not need healing. They need you. Many speak of the balancing, the clearing, the harmonising, the awakening, the opening, and the closing of these Sacred Gateways and energy centres. These Sacred Centres, dear ones, require one thing, and one thing only: They need your Love, dear ones, and when they receive your Love, they will manifest this into Light, and when Light is made manifest within these Sacred Gateways, everything within them will be brought back into perfection, and into its Divine Essence.

Your Diamond Lights will become self-healing, self-balancing and, once you place the seed of Love within them, that seed will burst forth into Light, and illuminate the Sacred Void of the Unmanifest. And within that Sacred Void of the Unmanifest, more Love will be created, so more Light will be created, and you will return back into the pure channel of Love that you have always been.

Everything within your Universe has been of service to you, has been willing to be channelled through you, and be transformed into energy – even of anger, confusion, doubt and fear. However, now these Grand Beings of Consciousness that you call your Planets are expanding, and opening their own Hearts and Souls, they are themselves returning to channels of pure Love. So, to keep yourselves in the dark, dear ones, to keep these Sacred Centres hidden from Love, will only bring you pain, illusion and disease, for this Universe cannot support your Sacred Journey of Illusion any longer. You cannot rely on them to assist you in the channelling of your pain and fear for they, like you, are now releasing Time from their consciousness. They have played the Sacred Game of Illusion, but now they return back into the Sacred Truth of Love.

Your Astrology and Astronomy will go through great changes, and many mystics will be given new concepts. For, dear ones, you are now in the New World, your Solar System is in the New World, your Universe is in the New World, and the Union of many Grand Consciousnesses is taking place.

Fill your Diamond Lights with the Love within your Heart and, with the Wisdom within your Soul, you shall release effortlessly and gracefully, the energies and experiences that now need to remain in the world of illusion, the Old World.

Ask us, the Union, to assist you, to support you, for you are multi-dimensional Beings of Light, and you are the Cosmic Consciousness of Love. You are the pioneers into the New World, the world of Diamond Light, the world of radiant remembrance, the world of your purity and innocence, the Cosmic Dance of your purpose, passion and play.

BEYOND THE LIGHT
'DARION'

We, the Union of Love, and we, the Union of Light, we re-acquaint you now with the essence, the Love and the desire of Darion, for he will teach you many things in these following Scriptions, that now need to be understood in your Unlimited Timelessness.

I, Darion, now carry myself forth on the vehicle of Light. I, Darion, now open my Heart to you, the loved, and the beloved of the New World. The essence of your Light, the Divinity of its radiations, brings great desire to allow you to be inspired, and to expand. I, Darion, like many of you on your Earthwalk have, if you choose, played with words, danced with vibrations, and enhanced and created many changes within these words, which by the way, in their very essence, are vibrations. So, when I speak of my name as 'Darion', I joyfully play with purpose, and as seen before you now, expand the name into two vibrations:

DAR - ION

I wish it to be known, with Joy and laughter, that I am what you may call the 'Dark Spark'. I am the Dark in Union with the Light. For an 'ION' is the Life-Force of Light, and what I am asking you to receive now, is one of the grandest Truths for any time, any space, or any civilization for that matter. The vehicle of Light that I express, the 'ION' of Life-Spark has, dear ones, been created from the Sacred Darkness and, as we have expressed to you in other Scriptions, Light is the physical manifestation of Love. Light, if you choose to see it this way, is an ultraviolet vibration, a Pure White Ray.

UNION OF SACRED DARKNESS & DIVINE LIGHT

Love, dear ones, Love is the Sacred Blackness of No-Thing, and of All Creation. Love cannot be contained within boundaries, within conditions, within designs. The very presence of Love is the foundation of All Creation, and is of such pure energy that it has in Hueman interpretation, no vibration, no sound.

Love Is - Love does not begin - Love does not end

INFINITE SOURCE

Love Is - Infinite Source - experiencing Itself

So, for your Hueman understanding, we now wish to give you two symbols, two energies, that will assist in the integration of such a teaching.

You may embrace Love, if you will, as a Sacred Black Ray and, when that Sacred Black Ray gives expression of itself, allows itself to manifest through Divine action, the Divine Light of the White Ray is created. And within the Divine White Ray of Light is your Rainbow, within your White Ray of Light is your Life-Force, your Spark, your experience, and your expansion.

We are asking you now to reach deeper, deeper into the very essence of your being, for within you is a Sacred Darkness, inexplicable, unlimited, and pure beyond your comprehension. It is the birthplace of your Spirit and Soul. It is the very foundation of All That Is, and it is even beyond I, Darion, the 'Dark Spark', to express to you its essence, or its creation. I can, however, tell you that it is my Home, it is the very Heart Of My Essence, and dear ones, it is also the very Heart of your essence, of your birthplace and, of course, your birthright.

Within this Sacred Black Ray of Love is a peace, is a place of unspeakable beauty and tenderness. I open this forth to you now, for when Union of the Sacred Darkness and the Divine Light is made manifest within your consciousness, within your being, the Joy and bliss you shall experience will also be of such beauty and such magnitude that you shall find yourselves speechless to express the experience of such a Union. I now wish, in this most Sacred of Scriptions, to gift you with another teaching, which, if you were not ready to receive, could not be expressed.

Understand, dear ones, both the Black and White Rays of All Creation lay deep within you, as you. Your Souls, the vehicles of your Spirit, the vehicles of the Sacred Darkness, carry within them this Sacred Black Ray of Love. And, as the Soul experiences the Hueman plane of consciousness, the very experience creates the White Ray of Divine Light, and this, dear ones, may be seen in the radiant Light of your Hearts.

Many have spoken of the 'Dark Night of the Soul', and all of you have or will experience this. And many of you, as you read this, will feel you are in such a night. Understand that what you call 'The Dark Night of the Soul' is simply the Soul beginning to remember its true Home, but through the fear of the Ego, and its resistance to surrender to the journey of the Soul, huge conflict is created within, and what you would call negative charge is released into the experience of the Soul, the Mind and, of course, the Body.

Many of you have been taught to seek 'The Light', and to reject the Darkness. Many of you have spent years searching for Light, and seeking the experience of Love, however, it is this very quest for Light that, may we say, keeps many of you entertained, and many of you deluded. For, in seeking the experience of Light, your society has become addicted purely to the experience. For it is in the silence and stillness of your existence that the very presence of Love may be felt.

Understand, to seek the Light as your saviour, to seek the Light as your destination, shall only bring the need for more Light, and if we may play on your words, your search for the Light has had many of you chasing Rainbows.

The Light, dear ones, is not the destination. The Light is the vehicle back to Love. Do not stop at the Light, embrace the Light, and indeed, enjoy the Light, but we ask that *in-deed* you surrender to the Sacred Darkness, and the Sacred Void of Love.

We do not dispute that Light is an activation of Love, and that Light is a physical manifestation of Love, however, if you are truly 'homesick', you shall surrender to the Sacred Void, to the Unknown, to the Holy Black Ray of the Divine Mother, and return into the bliss from which you were birthed.

We shall now lovingly, truthfully and joyfully express to you through this chart of 'The Hueman Path of Union', the journey of your Souls back to Joy.

THE HUEMAN PATH OF UNION

SPIRITUAL GIFT	DIAMOND LIGHT	HUEMAN CHALLENGE
THE UNMANIFEST	10	CREATION
OBSERVATION	9	CONTAMINATION
INTEGRATION	8	CONDEMNATION
REALIZATION	7	ILLUSION
SURRENDER	6	RESISTANCE
TRANSFORMATION	5	CONFIRMATION
RESPONSIBILITY	4	PERSECUTION
INITIATION	3	CONFUSION
FOUNDATION	2	DESTRUCTION
UNIFICATION	1	SEPARATION

THE SACRED JOURNEY
OF THE BLACK AND
WHITE RAYS

I, Darion, with such purpose, pleasure and passion, now lay before you the Sacred Path of your very Soul, and the experimental and expansive journey of your very Hearts and Minds.

Allow this chart of the 'Hueman Path of Union', now set before you, to be seen as two Sacred Rays. The 'Path of Hueman Challenge', we ask you to remember, has been created from your Divine White Ray of Light, and we also ask you to remember that the 'Path of your Spiritual Gift' has been birthed from your Sacred Black Ray of Love. So, we wish you to perceive this Path of Union as a Union of your Sacred Black Ray, and your Divine White Ray. And we ask that you begin at your Diamond Light of Ten.

So, from the Sacred Black Ray of Love, of the UNMANIFEST, of Infinite Spirit, your Soul was CREATED. It was birthed into experience, into Light, and it was placed into the Divine Creation of your Universe.

As you OBSERVED the Universe in which you found yourself, *your desire* for experience and for Light placed you into the very consciousness of the Universe, and a CONTAMINATION of a kind began.

Through your willingness, as a Soul, to experience and expand, you began to INTEGRATE perceptions and judgements that were so different to the original perceptions of your Infinite Spirit, and the Love for its Soul. And, as your Soul arrived on the Earth plane, and took residence in its Hueman Temple, it felt CONDEMNED within it. You felt your Soul shrinking and suffocating, for it was not used to such solitary confinement.

As a result of your imprisonment within the Hueman form, you had the REALIZATION of the vastness and beauty of the world around you, but the ILLUSION of separateness from your surroundings began to take over your mind, began to take over your memory of Truth, and you SURRENDERED to your separateness, to feeling powerless, and to the Unknown.

However, the Hueman Challenge was not to resist this, but in the RESISTANCE, in the struggle, in the denial of your true Home of the Sacred Void, you began a TRANSFORMATION. You began a courageous journey back into your Heart, and your Heart CONFIRMED your Light, and you began to forget your darkness, the Sacred Darkness of your Soul, for you were blinded by the Light, and the feelings of the Heart.

As your Heart and its Light searched for more Light, you found yourself taking on RESPONSIBILITY, taking on burdens, to try and keep the Light alive, to make sure the darkness did not return, for you felt darkness was separate from you, and Light was The Way. Through your fear to keep the Light alive within your life, within your mind, your very Soul felt alone and completely separate from your Heart. It felt it was being PERSECUTED, so your Soul began a journey of pain, of disease, Light-time (lifetime) after Light-time, for your Soul felt unworthy of the Light in your Heart and a battle, if you choose, between Light and Dark began.

However, your Soul continued to scream at your Heart and Mind for recognition, and guided you into INITIATION, to go within, to find self, to find the Soul, to find your very existence and purpose. But once more a great battle began to take place, for as you began your journey of self-discovery, the CONFUSION of the Mind's Ego, the experi-mental aspect of your consciousness began to take over, and brought great conflict, between Ego and Soul, between Heart and Head.

In fear of more conflict, you laid down what you thought to be strong FOUNDATIONS for your life. You laid down rules and regulations, you laid down 'The Way', the way of fear and retribution in your society, and in your very cells. In the process, you also denied the peace of your Soul, and the passion of your Heart, and buried them deep within your being.

Once more, the Sacred Black Ray of Love wished to reawaken and embrace you, and you found your foundations being challenged. Through fear, you began to manifest DESTRUCTION, and you created war and disease, but then through the need for survival, you had to re-group, and wished once more for UNIFICATION. So new customs, beliefs, reforms, and revolutions of both your religious and material worlds were created to bring a false sense of oneness and unity.

Once again, dear ones, many of you find yourselves SEPARATE, alone and homesick. For, understand in this marriage, in this complication of misunderstanding, in this confused Union of the Divine White Ray of Light and the Sacred Black Ray of Love, all you have done is created 'shades of grey', fogs of consciousness, clouds of doubt, and lack of direction.

I, Darion, now wish you to see this Hueman Path of Union, this Union of Sacred Darkness and Divine Light in another way. For understand, the following teachings are very *Black and White*.

'SHADES OF GREY'

These 'Shades of Grey' of which I speak, also relate to what you would term between your ears, as 'grey matter'. For understand, dear ones, this grey matter can be your greatest friend or most powerful foe. It is time for you to understand its very creation, its very existence.

Many speak of getting past the barriers of the mind, but we wish you to understand exactly what the mind is. It is Divine in its Creation, of course, or it would not exist. This is Law. The mind, as you know, is a multi-faceted, multi-dimensional being in its own right, and many battles have taken place within the mind, and many grand decisions in your history have been made with the mind.

The Heart and Soul have sat back quietly, many times over, waiting for the mind to surrender, for the mind to understand that it is not on its own. Only within the Heart and the Soul do the Black and White Rays exist, the Divine White Ray of your Heart, and the Sacred Black Ray of your Soul. So, of course, the 'shades of grey' that we speak of can only be created in the mind. Once again in Joy, and with Divine purpose, we would like to play with your words.

I, Darion, now bring forth a word, a concept that has created much chaos, much drama, and much misconception. This grand word is your EGO, and this grand concept has been your doubt, has been your fear, has been your downfall. For there has been a great lack of understanding of what the EGO actually is, and what the EGO actually is not.

As a result of this lack of understanding, the shadow aspect of the EGO has taken over, for you have not looked past the veils of the doubts, and the fears that are created within the mind, within the grey matter. However, once understanding is complete within your being, the EGO shall become your friend, and not your foe. We now wish to give you a new perception, for which, once more, we feel you are ready. I, Darion, now place before you a Grand Truth indeed, and one which may take some time to actually comprehend, and truly understand. EGO, we wish you to understand, symbolically represents:-

EXPERI-MENTAL
GOD
ORDER

Know this: the Divine White Ray of Light is the Light of Action, of Male Force, of the Divine Father, and it is the Divine Father who wished through self-growth and expansion, to gift you with an Experi-mental God Order, or EGO. Father God wished you full self-expression, full freedom of expansion and experience, so that you may become your own Divine Creator and, through thought, to experience and experiment with anything you choose.

This, dear ones, is your EGO; the entity that allows you to do this. And, once you fully understand the dynamics, and the essence of the EGO, you may begin to work in harmony with it. As you now come into the New World of your own consciousness, you must understand this very important aspect of your 'grey matter' because, without this understanding, you will only create 'shades of grey', and lack of perception, and if you choose to perceive this another way, the Experi-mental God Order of your own consciousness would not exist without the permission and acceptance of your very Heart and Soul.

It is, of course, a Sacred Triad that has been misaligned, misused and misunderstood. And when the final piece of the puzzle is fully embraced by you, embraced by your EGO, then the Sacred Triad of your Soul, your Heart, and your Mind shall come into blissful Union, and become one Grand Consciousness of Love and Light. For, understand this

Truth: We have spoken to you of the New World, but now you must realise **YOU ARE THE NEW WORLD.**

The Re-Union of the Holy Triad is what will put it into place, and will allow you to go forth with a perception of such beauty, such Union, and such Joy. Then, as your understanding of the EGO moves into clarity, and moves into acceptance, it will allow you to fully embrace the Sacred Darkness, and the Divine Light.

As a Huemanity, dear ones, your Souls have travelled along the White Ray, through all the challenges, through all the grief, through all the separation, through all the doubt and all the fear. And now, as you stand alone, separate and lost, you are being asked to jump into the Black Ray of Love, into the Black Ray of Union, and Unification. For this is the path back to Joy!

Your Huemanity has travelled long and hard on this White Ray of experience, of experiment, and of expression, and it has been blessed by the Masculine Force of your Universe. However, now it is the Mother, the Sacred Feminine Force of Love that calls you back into Her Heart, and into your Home.

As you gaze upon this chart of Hueman Union, know that many Souls may be experiencing different aspects of the White or Black Rays but, as a Huemanity, you all stand on the edge of a cliff, and before you is the Abyss. Having for so long embraced the White Ray of Experience, you must now walk through the 'shades of grey', and release the illusion, for this is the Gateway, this is the Sacred Door, back into Union, back into the Divine Blackness of the mystery and the magnificence of your very Souls.

As we have expressed before, this does not mean that you leave your beautiful Earth, it means you come back into Union with your very Souls, with the Black Ray deep within your Hueman Temples. As we speak of your Hueman Temples, understand that the physical temples which rest gently and intentionally either side of your eyes, they too are the guardians of the EGO, of the Experi-mental God Order. These

Hueman physical temples are also Gateways, dear ones, into the Higher Consciousness of your Beings.

There are many Sacred Spaces, within your consciousness, that you are not aware of as yet, but they shall be revealed to the courageous Hearts who embrace the Black Ray of their Souls, the Black Ray of Love, the Black Ray of All Existence. For the Mother of Love is the Observer of All Existence, Love is the Giver of All Existence, Love is pure, in its perfection, and requires No-Thing.

That same No-Thing is your very Home, it is the Vast Void of Absolute Love, a Love so grand it cannot be contained in any form, other than Sacred Space. And you know this in your Hearts, for your Hearts have heard your Souls cry out, to allow the Black Ray of Love to wrap you in its Sacredness, in its silence, in its bliss.

We shall now share an exercise with you that I, Darion, the 'Dark Spark' have created to assist you in the grand Re-Union of the Holy Triad of your Being; the Triad, your Soul, your Heart and your Mind. All that is required by you for this exercise is your *pure intention*, and your *passionate desire* for Union with the Holy Triad within; the Triad of the Moon, the Sun and the Stars:

The Soul is the Triad of the Moon, the Soul is the Feminine, and is the physical manifestation of Love through the Hueman being.

The Heart is the Triad of the Sun, the Heart is the Masculine, and is the expression of Love through radiant Light.

The Mind is the Triad of the Stars, the Mind is both Masculine and Feminine in essence, and is the Initiate of All Creation.

RE-UNION EXERCISE OF HEART, MIND AND SOUL

Find yourself a silent, Sacred space. Rest your body in darkness and have before you a single flame of Light.

1. With eyes closed and imagination open, bring your awareness to the **Diamond Light of your Four**, the Sacred Sanctuary of your Soul, and perceive within it a small Black Ray of Light.

2. Allow this to radiate through this Sacred space of your Hueman Temple, and see deep within the Black Ray, a soft blue light.

3. Now, take a few moments to feel the presence and Love of the Mother of All Creation. Feel Her wrap Her Black Ray of Love around your very Soul, bringing it purification, and peace.

4. Now, draw your awareness up to the Sacred House of your Heart, the **Diamond Light of your Five**, and perceive, within it, the Divine Flame of the White Ray. Allow this to radiate

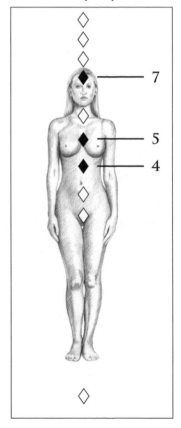

through this Divine Space of your Hueman body, and see emanating from the White Ray, a soft golden light.

5. Now, take a few moments to feel the Light of the Father of All Experience. Feel Him fill your Heart and Divine Flame with His purpose and passion for you, and your living.

6. Bringing your awareness to the Sacred Realm of your Mind, the **Diamond Light of Seven,** perceive now, either side of this centre, in the area of your temples, the Sacred Black Ray of the Mother upon the left temple, and the Divine White Ray of the Father upon the right. Allow their presence to gently pulse for a few moments within each temple, for your temples are the Sacred Doorways into your Higher Consciousness, and your Experi-mental God Order.

7. Now, see within the centre of your Mind, these Black and White Rays coming into Union, and witness being birthed from them a radiant red figure Eight. For Red is the Ray of All Manifestation, and All Manifestation is Sac-red. Allow this Red Infinity Symbol to gently pulse and rotate for a few moments within the Sacred Realm of your Mind.

8. When you are ready, you may release and rest the Red Ray of Eight upon your head, for it will continue to bring the peace, the passion, and the perceptions of your Hueman being into perfect Union.

9. You may then breathe in the golden light of the candle within your room, and bring yourself back into full consciousness.

Repeat this exercise as often, or as little as you choose, for you have always been the Masters of your own destiny. Make it a destiny of Joy, make it a destiny of Love and Light, and allow the shades of grey to dissolve, and to return back into the Love and Light of your being.

I, Darion, now wish to leave you with some 'food for thought' that has been covered with lashings of luscious Truth.

THOUGHT + TIME = EGO

EGO + LIGHT = HIGHER CONSCIOUSNESS

HIGHER CONSCIOUSNESS + LOVE = JOY

RIVER OF STARS

We, the Union of Love, and we, the Union of Light, praise you for your willingness to open your Sacred consciousness to such Scriptions, to such perceptions, to such analysis. For, understand, dear Hearts and grand Souls, that, as we speak of your Universe and your Planets being present within the Sacred Gateways of your being, understand that your consciousness is reflected through the radiance and magnificence of the Stars, of the Galaxies, of the Milky Way and Beyond. Your consciousness *are* the Star Systems, *are* the Galaxies, *are* the Gateways, and *are* the River of Stars.

When we speak of the EGO, the Experi-mental God Order, we speak of a grand gift indeed, for we speak of a gift that we know will be understood, will be embraced, and will bring great Joy to the mind and the magnificent Light within it. For, understand this, the Pineal gland which could be termed a master cell of your being, and that we wish to call a 'Supernova' of your consciousness, is in direct alignment with your Milky Way, your River of Stars. For the Milky Way is a transmitter, a receiver, and is a Grand Being in its own right.

Within your own Pineal gland is this same River of Stars, this Ocean of Grand Consciousness. And if you choose, at any moment of your being, you may go within and reflect, and ask that this Sacred River of Stars be activated and initiated within this Supernova of your mind, within the very Heart of your thought systems. And because the Pineal gland is so expansive, the Experi-mental God Order was created to contain it in your time and space, so that your Hueman perception may receive and transmit, *safely* and *creatively*, but also understand *expansively* the energies within it, the Divine Creation around it, and the magnificent glory of its existence.

Many great minds upon your Earth have initiated this Supernova of their being. They have connected to the Universe, and received many Truths that others in Huemanity could not receive. Each of you have within you this gift, and it is the balance between the Supernova consciousness of your Pineal gland and the Experi-mental God Order of your mind, that now must come into harmony, into grace, into Union.

All thought is a Starseed for Creation, and you hold within your very centre of thought systems, a magnificent Star indeed, a Supernova of Grand Consciousness, so understand, dear ones, your quest for illumination has kept you fixed on the Divine White Ray of Light, and for thousands of years you have travelled with the Masculine Force, with the Divine White Ray. Many of your original teachings of Spirit, of God, have allowed only the Light to exist, for in your very teachings, God said, 'Let there be Light'.

As we have said, God is the Light, the Masculine Force of Life, of Action, and of Divine Will, hence, some Hueman beings have come into Union with this Supernova of your mind, and many have danced around it, whilst others have become unbalanced within the Experi-mental God Order, the Ego. For thought creates experience, thought is Will, thought creates Life-Force, and thought creates Death Force. So thought, in Truth, is Male in its aspect, and in its action.

You, dear ones, have experienced many Light-times of the Male aspect, and this has been grand and beautiful, in its own right. However, in many, many of your societies, you have turned your backs on the Female Force of Darkness. You have perceived it as wicked, as something to fear. For even though a Male may initiate a Starseed of Creation, it is the Female who births Life. It is the Sacred Darkness of the womb where all Life begins, whether it be a Hueman infant in the Mother's womb, or a seedling in your Mother Earth. All are birthed from Darkness.

Before your White Ray of living, of civilization, of experience, there were many Ancients who lived on your Earth within the Black Ray of Love, embracing the Darkness and fullness of the Mother; of the Female Force. You may look through many of your History books to see how and where this began, and ended. But as you know, everything is cyclic and, as we have explained, you are all now ready, as a Huemanity, to once more return to the Sacred Black Ray of Love, of being, of nurturing, of purity. For She is back, She is Sacred, Holy and Eternal, and no matter what your Light experience, all Souls return to Her. She wishes to come into full Union with the experience of Light, with the Male Force, and with you. It is difficult for us, the Union, to express the simplicity and the complexity of these teachings, so we ask that you receive them intentionally, through the Supernova of your Mind, the remembrance of your Soul, and the willingness of your Heart.

She, the Mother, has returned into your being, into your consciousness, and into your Earth, and you shall know this now, through any physical disharmony and dysfunction of your very bodies, emotions and minds. For, the Love of the Sacred Black Ray, the Gift of the Mother, cannot be given, it can only be surrendered to, and any resistance on your part will bring the dysfunctions and disharmonies of which we speak.

Love is not a Force, as the Divine White Ray of Light is a Force. Love is not an action, it is not an experience, and it definitely is not an experiment. Of course, you experience Love through Light, you manifest Love through Light, and the Male Force has shown you this many times over, but Love requires no action, no movement, no direction. For, as we have said, Love is within All Existence, and everything that exists is, in Truth, the very purity, power, and majesty of Love. However, in the Experi-mental God Order, in the gift of Self Creation, you, dear ones, have simply forgotten the Love within All Existence. Understand this:

LOVE IS THE LAW. LIGHT IS THE WAY

When you can fully embrace this Truth, you shall not be able to contain your Joy, you shall not be able to remain in illusion, and you shall not be able to create fear. Light and Love are now coming back into the ONE HEART, the ONE CREATION, the ONE JOY. Love and Light wish for your UNION with them, for you, dear ones, are their greatest JOY, their greatest LIGHT, and their greatest LOVE.

REVELATIONS

I, Shalamar, now come forth in Light and with Love to bring you more revelations. For a revelation is a blissful moment of Truth, and a revelation can bring the Ego and the Supernova of your consciousness into balance, into harmony, and into Union.

We believe in all beliefs, for all beliefs lead back to the One Truth, no matter how long and winding the path may be, on the road of beliefs. All shall lead back to the Truth, so we do not dispute any teachings to this point, for if the intention is pure, the Truth shall stand strong.

We now wish to share with you an idea, a concept that we feel is of great wonder, and brings us, and hopefully you, much excitement. For, as we have spoken of the New World, the World of Joy, we would like to bring your attention to an Ancient Scripture, that holds within it, pure Truth. We speak of your Bible, a book of huge proportions, a book of great guidance, and we wish to draw your attention to the Scriptures of 'Revelation', for, dear Hearts and wondrous Souls, we can see the great Truth within the words. For 'Revelation' speaks of 'The End', the end of suffering, and the end of separation, however, we would like to add a little twist to the interpretation, and a slight change to the perception. Within these pages of your Bible, it speaks of the Apocalypse, of the Fall, of the Four Horsemen. It also speaks of famine, of disease, and many things that bring fear to the Hueman race.

Love, expressed as the Sacred Black Ray, is re-awakening within your Universe, within your Earth, and within your own being, and as expressed, Love cannot have boundaries, and requires only Sacred Space within which to exist. However, in your consciousness and within your beings, you have pushed Love away. You have tried to contain Her, you have tried to control Her, to manipulate Her, and even to defame Her. The Apocalypse, dear ones, is simply the return of denied Love, of denied feeling, of the denied Feminine, and the denial of your very Souls.

The Four Horsemen are the four elements of Fire, of Water, of Air, and of Earth. Within each Hueman being are these four elements; within your Earth are these four elements; within your Nature are these four elements; and within your Universe, spiritually speaking, are these four elements. They are the four dimensions of your being, and they exist within those four Sacred Chambers of your Heart, of your Sun. Love shall be known within your Soul, and be expressed through the four elements of your Being, of your Earth, of your Universe, and of your Nature.

The Apocalypse is not the Light of God's Will returning, it is the Sacred Black Ray of the Mother, for She shall not be denied any longer. She shall not be shunned or destroyed. For, understand, what many of you perceive as the 'Black Mother', as the Destroyer, as the Feminine Force of Nature, has simply been expressing your denial of Her. This denial has been made manifest by the Will, the Light and the Action of the Male Force. She is no greater than He, but Her Existence of Love shall not be denied any longer. This, dear ones, in this 'Revelation', is the Grand Truth, which shall birth the New World of Joy within you and all your surroundings.

The Garden of Eden, as it were, never disappeared. It was only clouded by your 'shades of grey', by your fear and your perception of separation and abandonment. The Garden of Eden is the Sacred Black Ray of Love within your Soul, coming into Union with the Divine White Ray of your Heart. You may see your Heart as the 'Adam' and your Soul as the 'Eve', for the Sacred Black Ray is on the Eve of Full Expression, is on the Brink of Revelation, and within your society, know this: the Black and White races of your civilizations will only come into Union when the Black and White Rays, within the self, come into Re-Union.

The Ancient Ancestors of your world wait patiently for your Revelation, for your revealing of the Truth, for in the New World of Joy there is no separation, there is no abandonment, and there is no fear. I, Shalamar, I, of the Rose Red Ray, wish all to know, whether they be black or white of origin, that the same Red Ray of All Manifestation courses through your veins, and we thank you for sharing with us the Sacred Space of your consciousness, of your River of Stars.

THE CIRCLE OF LIFE

We, the Union of Love, and we, the Union of Light, we come forth, we come now, to bring before you, to reawaken within you, our Ancient Brothers and Sisters, your very heritage of purity and Truth. For all has come full cycle, dear ones, and you shall find yourselves back at the beginning, back to your purity, back to your innocence, back into the Majesty of your Being and your Becoming.

To resist this beginning, this becoming, this Grand Awakening, is your choice, your desire, and understand, possibly your purpose at this time. If the mind is not ready to surrender to the Soul's journey, then may we suggest, no judgement be placed upon this, no judgement of self, no anger of self, for this will only hold up your journey further, dear ones.

Each and every Soul, when its Divine destiny allows, shall leave, what we call, the karmic grid-lock of Huemanity, and shall burst forth into the Cosmic Consciousness, into the River of Stars, that lays nestled, waiting in your 'shades of grey' – in your mind. For when the mind does surrender to the Soul, when the shades of grey dissolve back into the Black and White Rays of Existence and Experience, the River of Stars, this Supernova of your consciousness shall burst forth, and you shall have the realization, and revelation of Grand Union with All Existence. And there shall be no karma, there shall be no judgement. For karma has just been a tool to assist you in the journey of your judgements, of your illusions, and of your separation.

The Ancient Brothers and Sisters of whom we speak, their River of Stars, shone brightly, danced freely, and experienced Oneness, for they had not yet discovered their Experi-mental God Order. They wish to speak now, they wish to fill you with desire, with passion and with peace, for the journey back to the beginning, back into their arms, their Hearts and their Souls. The Spirit, the Will, and the Heart of a Great Elder, a pure Ancient One, now wishes to be in communion with you, and the name of this true Spirit is Shenekah.

I, Shenekah, come to you in full Heart, in full desire, in full purpose and in full peace. I, Shenekah, now come before you, my Brothers and my Sisters, to greet you with harmony, and to greet you with the Love of the Black Ray.

I come forward now, and speak on behalf of all my Brothers and my Sisters, for we have observed your journey, we have observed your chaos, your crises, and your commitment to avoid yourselves. Understand: all that you are *missing* is within YOU; all that you *desire* is within YOU; all that you *ache* for is within YOU; and all that you *need* is within YOU.

My Tribes, my people, their desires were few, their needs were none, but their purpose was grand and filled with passion, for in the experience of this Hueman existence, they knew the Joy of Union with such a Grand Being of Consciousness as our Earth. Such a Female Force of breathtaking beauty, of sheer delight, of rapturous and voluptuous presence; and we travelled, we walked, we climbed, and we swam through her Being, and around her Being, until we became One with her.

For, know this Truth as we knew this Truth: Our Earth is a daughter of the God and the Goddess of this Creation, and her purity, her innocence, her peace and her passion, pulse through every living thing that she births. Your Nature is the very manifestation of her Joy.

The Tribes of which I speak, these Tribes were birthed in the Great Southern Lands, and the Great Southern Lands have separated themselves, as did our Tribes, and as do yours. They broke away, they left their original beginning, and many of what you call your Continents. They are all Brothers and Sisters, but they have great oceans of separateness between themselves and your Earth, the Daughter of All Creation. She, too, feels separate, for her Brothers and Sisters are the Planets, and there are, between them, great oceans of Stars and Galaxies.

But, know this, my Brothers and my Sisters, to remember the Oneness and the Union with yourselves, with each other, and with us, will allow a wave of Consciousness to be re-born, a Consciousness of Oneness, a Consciousness of Union, a Consciousness of Peace.

We, the Ancient Ones, reside in you, as you. We began this journey of separateness, and now you shall complete it, and it is with great reverence that I, Shenekah, speak for all my people, when we bless you with our gratitude. For this last leg of the journey has been a most desperate one, indeed, a most difficult and dangerous cycle from separateness back into Unity.

Through your pure Desire and Will, it shall be done, and we, the Ancients, walk within you, and beside you. We send you our Courage; the Consciousness of our Age. To urge you, we send you our Desire, we send you our Love, we plead with you, we beg you to allow the Sacred Black Ray of Love to be remembered, to be re-birthed, and to be reunited within you and within us.

Your Mayan culture, which was a culture not yet in our perception, was correct when they told you the Great Circle, the Great Circle back to Oneness, will be completed. For this daughter of the God and the Goddess, she is remembering, she is remembering her Oneness with her Brothers and her Sisters, and she cannot wait for your remembrance anymore.

She wishes with all her Heart to be in Union with you, her Brothers and her Sisters, for that is what you are. She wishes to be in Union with all her family, and her Heart aches for your remembrance, as ours does, but only you can take that leap of faith, back into remembrance, back into Oneness.

The great Circle of Life is upon us, do not waste another breath in separateness and despair. Call upon us, the Ancients, to assist you in the remembrance of your innocence and your purity. We wait patiently for you to return, and we shall not abandon you, for the great Circle of Life is spinning very fast, and only in Union can we complete the journey back into the One Heart, back into the One Spirit.

We, the Ancient Ones, know you as the Brave Hearts. This is what we call you, for this is what you are. With Love, we send you our Courage, our Commitment, our Consciousness, and our River of Stars, so they may Light your way back to the beginning of your Joy, and your very Existence.

THE MYSTERY
AND THE MAJESTY

We, the Union of Love, and we, the Union of Light, we, the Guardians of your Sacred Universe, we wish it to be known that we are in conscious Union with the Guardians of your Earth, your Ancient Ones. And we wish it to be known that we are in conscious Union with the Guardians of your Star Systems, the Star Elders of your Universe.

Understand this next concept to the best of your perception; the Three Temples of Light within your being are also in communion with these Guardians, of which we speak:

The Sacred Temple of your Moonlight, of your Soul's Earth cycle, this Temple is in communion with the Ancient Ones of your Earth.

The Sacred Temple of your Sunlight, of your Heart's experience of Truth, this Temple is in communion with the Star Elders of your Universe.

The Sacred Temple of your Starlight, of your God/Goddess consciousness, this Temple is in communion with us, the Union of Love and Light.

We now wish to clarify what we believe a Guardian to be. The intent of a Guardian is to serve, to nourish, and to guide, and a Guardian holds within them all the knowledge of the energetic aspects of that which it serves.

It is time for you to accept, in Truth, in fact, that you are all energetic aspects of the Ancient Ones of your Earth, and the Star Elders of your Universe, and that you are all energetic aspects of us, the Union of Love, and the Union of Light. For, we could not be in communion with you unless an aspect of us was an aspect of you.

We, the Union, we, the Star Elders, and we, the Ancient Ones, in Love and service to you, we have made a commitment. We have made a commitment to serve, to nourish, and to guide; to serve you with Love, to nourish you with Knowledge, and to guide you with Light. In the giving of these gifts of Guardianship, we become Love, we awaken to Knowledge, we experience Light, and we feel Joy and Union with All Creation. And it is our very commitment to you, it is our Love for you that allows the very beauty, majesty, and mystery of this Universe to continue to expand, and to experience.

We ask you now, in our Love for you, to give *yourself* the same commitment, the same honour, the same Love and nurturing that has been our greatest pleasure to give you. We ask that you make a commitment to your journey, and to your Joy. For understand, a commitment is a Sacred Marriage of energies, the energies of desire and intention coming into the Union of completion. For, in completion, there is Oneness, and in Oneness there is All Existence, and All Existence lays within you, and we, like the Ancients and the Elders, have always known this as Truth.

We do not demand anything of you, but we do suggest that you allow *yourselves* the gift of *yourselves*, the majesty and the mystery of *yourselves*. For commitment is the key to your Sacred journey of the Eternal peace, passion, purpose and play that lies deep within all beings.

Many may ask, how do I make this commitment, and find this key to my journey for, in Truth, if you are mystery, how can you commit to self, how can you find the way Home to the Heart of your essence? This, dear ones, is what makes Eternity such a Joy, for the path of Eternity is the grandest mystery of all knowledge, and it is the very presence, and the essence of mystery that allows Eternity to become!

So, to commit to yourself is to commit to the mystery, and the majesty of your Being, and your Eternal Becoming. For, understand the "I AM' of your Being is in Truth:

> **INFINITE**
> **ABSOLUTE**
> **MYSTERY**

We understand that the Experi-mental God Order may have difficulty with this perception. However, allow the Supernova of your consciousness to show you the way to such a Truth.

So, in essence, we are asking you to commit to the Unknown. We are asking you to step into the world of your Ancient Ones; we are asking you to experience the Universe of your Star Brothers and Sisters; and we are asking you to remember us, the Union of Love and Light, who lay just beyond your Universe, and who guard and serve your Eternal Being.

We wish to present you with a text that we consider to be as Sacred now, as it was considered to be many thousands of years ago, and once more, we wish to use as a foundation, the Spiritual teachings of your Bible, in order to open you to a concept, and to awaken you to a consciousness that we know you are ready to receive.

As we have said in previous Scriptions, Love is the Law, Love is the Law of All Existence, for All Existence is Love; and we understand that at certain points of your history, of your White Ray experience, Laws of an Earthly nature were required, and we perceive that some of these grandest of Laws were written in your Ten Commandments, in the Ten Commandments of the Bible.

In this time of your history that they were scribed, it was understandable as to why they were required, and they have served a purpose. Know this, the Ten Commandments were of service to Huemanity, for their intention was to serve, nourish, and guide the very beings for which they were written.

We now wish, with the greatest reverence, to add, if you choose, a new dimension to such Laws. For, in Truth, they were teachings on how to honour, serve, and protect *one another*. However, what we wish to set before you now, is guidance on how to Love, honour, serve and nourish *yourselves*.

In having full responsibility for self, you shall find your gifts, and when you give of your gifts, you become a Joy to the World; you give back to the Earth that has given to you, you honour your Brothers and your Sisters, and you become One with All Creation.

For this Divine purpose, we wish to use the Ten Diamond Lights within your Hueman Temples, for they not only express all aspects of your Universe, they also hold within them the majesty and the mystery of Eternity.

We also wish to give you Ten Keys, and we wish these to be known as the Ten Commitments, the Ten Commitments to Self, the Ten Commitments to Serve, the Ten Commitments of your Soul. Each one of these Ten Keys, these Ten Commitments, is a Guardian at a Gateway to the mystery and the majesty of your Ten Diamond Lights.

When you re-awaken and activate each Commitment, your Diamond Lights shall burst forth in magnificence, and you shall not need to seek anything outside of yourself. You shall become all that you desire. You shall wrap yourself around yourself, in complete Union, in complete Love, and experience the Light of your Divine Radiance.

In the following Scriptions, the Star Elders of your Universe shall come forth, and assist you in the Revelations of the Commitments for which your Souls, Hearts, and Minds have ached for Aeons. Know this: a Commitment is the action of communion, and communion with All Creation is your birthright, and is your path to Joy.

THE TEN
COMMITMENTS

10. I am All with the Mystery of the Goddess, and I am One with the Majesty of God.

9. I am Eternal Spirit.

8. I am in communion with All Creation.

7. I create Infinite Experience.

6. I surrender to my Divine Will.

5. I experience the Light of my Heart.

4. I accept the guidance of my Soul.

3. I honour all my emotions.

2. I nourish my Hueman Temple.

1. I Serve Mother Earth with my gifts.

THE CRYSTAL BALL

As we have spoken, and as we have explained, we have been making a very deep connection with your Inner Worlds, with your Inner Realms, and with your Diamond Lights. We, the Union of Love, and we, the Union of Light, have described to you our position in your perception. We have told you of the Auroradei, we have told you where we reside, and of the magnificent energy of mystery around your Universe for, if you imagine your Universe as a Crystal Ball, we reside in the Auric Field, the Auroradei, around that Crystal Ball and, as we look within, we see all things. We see you, dear ones, with great clarity. We see you as beings of such beauty, and we see you, dear ones, as multi-dimensional beings of such grand mystery, and majesty.

As we look closely into this Crystal Ball, into this Universe, we see many parts to the whole. We see the Planets, the Galaxies, and the Gateways, and even though, in your perception, it may appear that you are only part of this whole, magnificent Crystal Ball, in Truth:

YOU ARE THE CRYSTAL BALL.

You are everything within the Crystal Ball, and in Truth, it is your Experi-mental God Order that has allowed you to separate yourself from yourself, to separate yourself from your Crystal Ball and from your Universe, so that you may perceive a unique aspect of it, and this, of course, is Truth also.

As in your time, and space, and reality, you are experiencing a unique aspect within that Crystal Ball, you must now come to realise that:

YOU ARE ALL OF THE CRYSTAL BALL

We watch in such awe, and we watch in such gratitude, for your willingness to separate yourself from yourself, to live, if you choose, in such a concentrated vibration of one unique aspect. As we have said, it is only the ability and courage of a Master, that could achieve this concentrated, unique experience of itself.

For, everything you perceive outside of yourself, is *yourself*, and it has been your illusion of separateness that has caused your struggle, your sorrow, and your selfishness. And we, the Union, who are One with the Auroradei, this outer shell of your Crystal Ball, of your Universe, we wish it to be known, that as everything outside of you is also within you, so, too, the Auroradei is a Divine aspect of your Being.

If we were to explain this Sacred Space of majesty and mystery to you, for your perception, we would describe it as an opalescent silver blue ocean of Love, and as a radiant, silver blue ray of Re-Union. This silver blue ray of Re-Union, of remembrance, exists around the outer shell of your Auric Fields, your 'Shells of Light'. It is the silver blue ray of our Consciousness, and if we were to add a new dimension to this silver blue ray, it would be one of such Light and such Darkness, for both exist in the one Eternal Moment.

The Auroradei of which we speak is the existence of Love, and the experience of that Love, all in one Eternal Moment. And somewhere, within your cells, you shall remember this vision, for every Soul has been here, in this Auroradei of Consciousness. It is time for you to realise that within you are multi-dimensional worlds, as around you there are multi-dimensional worlds, and that there has been a 'War of the Worlds' within each and every Hueman Temple, at some point of the journey.

Understand, the only reason for this 'War of the Worlds', is that these multi-dimensional worlds within and around you have not been given acknowledgement, acceptance, and understanding, and, as you have created a 'War of the Worlds' within you, throughout your Hueman history, you have also created a 'War of the Worlds' around you. But the

'War of the Worlds' around you is not the problem, it is the battle *within* that creates the battle *with-out!* So, grasp the concept, the perception, the Truth, that everything *around you*, whether you like it or not, is also *within you*, and that all these worlds, all these Diamond Light Gateways ask of you, is your recognition, your understanding, and your Love:

THIS IS WHERE HUEMANITY NOW STANDS!

Nothing outside of yourself shall give you any true solutions. You can search many Light-times over for them, and many illusionary answers shall appear, with those answers creating no more than the need for more solutions. In Truth, you have arrived on this Planet, at this time, to take a Hueman leap of faith through the Veils of Illusion back into the Love, the Truth, and the Joy of All Existence.

The only way you may come into Union with your Inner Worlds, with your Diamond Lights, is to commit to them, to serve, to nourish, and to honour them. The Ten Commitments have been gifted to you so that you may walk through the Gateway of Illusion, back into the Worlds of Illumination, back into the Sacred Worlds of your own Being, back into the Mystery and Majesty of your Becoming.

THAT WHICH SINGS

AND CONTEMPLATES IN

YOU IS STILL DWELLING

WITHIN THE BOUNDS OF

THAT FIRST MOMENT

WHICH SCATTERED

THE STARS INTO SPACE

KAHIL GIBRAN

MESSAGE OF
THE STAR ELDERS

With great reverence, we now invite the Star Elders of your Universe to come forward and be in communion with you, their Brothers and their Sisters.

I speak now as one of the Star Elders. I come forth, in Love and gratitude for your willingness to be in Union with us. We wish you to understand, as there is the Holy Triad within your own being, there is also the Holy Triad of your Universe which includes:-

The Ancient Ones of your Earth,
and her Brothers and Sisters, the Planets.

The Guardians of your Universe,
the Union of Love and Light.

And we, the Star Elders of your Star Systems,
with their Galaxies and Gateways.

Together, we form an alliance, and we are a Triad of Love, not just for you, dear ones, but also for us. For, understand, we are also in the process of evolution, of expanding our own consciousness, and we wish to come to you to explain and reveal some Truths that have been held back for many of your Earth's revolutions.

We, the Star Elders, at the beginning of your Earth's birth, and at the very beginning of your Huemanity, were in direct communion with the Ancient Ones of your Mother Earth, and her surrounding Planets of Grand Consciousness. There was much Joy, there was much Light, and existence flourished, for it was Love. We have watched over your Earth for many of her revolutions, and we, too, have been in awe for, understand this:

IN YOUR HUEMAN FORM YOU ARE UNIQUE.
THERE ARE NO OTHER BEINGS LIKE YOU ANYWHERE, IN ANY REALM.

We are aware that your consciousness has perceived us, the Star Elders, as also unique and sometimes frightening, but we are only frightening, dear ones, for that has been the programming put upon your minds by those who wished to hold power and control over your mass consciousness. Many stories of fear and untruths have been placed upon your Planet, and this brings great sadness to our perceptions.

For, understand, as the Star Elders, we have not been gifted with the expression of emotion. We are allowed to feel, we are allowed to think, however, the Source of All Creation, at this point of our journey, has only allowed our Sacred Heart Centres to express at an elementary level.

As we witness the depth of emotion you can experience and express, we find ourselves speechless and unable to conceptualise, within thought, that which we witness. For, we see from a detached perception, how powerful and potent the emotional being you possess can be. We see how creative, and how destructive it can be, and we wish you to know this Truth:

YOUR EMOTIONS AND THEIR EXPRESSIONS ARE
THE MOST POWERFUL FORCE IN THIS UNIVERSE!

We, as Star Nations, have been perceived, in Truth, as being mentally and intellectually advanced when compared to your Hueman Race, and in many aspects, this is so. But, even with our advanced body of knowledge, this pales into insignificance when compared with the force of energy that is created through the emotional being of your Hueman

Temples, and you must come to understand the force of this emotional being that has been gifted to you.

The Experi-mental God Order, which you have been given, has allowed you, through many trials and tribulations, to also experience the highs and lows of your emotional being, and the excesses and illusions of the Experi-mental God Order has allowed you the experience of all emotions, whether they appear positive or negative in expression. Once you accept and embrace this emotional being and becoming, of feeling, of expression, of manifestation, once you honour it, once you nourish it, you shall find your power, your purpose, and your passion. For, understand, the Star Elders watch you very closely.

As you evolve, so do we, and understand this: there are four worlds within your Heart; there are four elements within your nature and your physical being; and there are also four Key Civilisations of your Universe.

Firstly, there is the Grand Civilisation of your Universe, and the Guardians from its beginning, the Union of Love and Light. There is the Civilisation of your Stars, with we the Star Elders, the Guardians of your Galaxies. There is the Civilisation of your Ancients, the Guardians of your Earth, and surrounding Planets, and there is you, the Hueman Civilisation.

You are the Guardians of the most powerful force in the Universe, the Force of Emotion; *the expression of Gods' experience.* And to perceive this another way: the Ancient Ones are the originals of the Physical Realm, the element of Earth; we, the Star Elders are the originals of the Mental Realm, the element of Air; and the Union of Love and Light are the originals of the Spiritual Realm, the element of Fire.

However, you, dear ones, are all these elements, and more. It is now the Hueman Civilisation that leads the way in our evolution. As the originals of the Emotional Realm, the element of Water, you alone are the ones experiencing the combined force of the Physical, Mental, Spiritual, and Emotional Realms.

We wait for you to lead the way. We wait for you to liberate the Ancient Ones from their Earth grids. We wait for you to liberate us, the Star Elders from the labyrinth of our intellect. And the Union of Love and Light wait for you to bring us all back into pure Spirit, pure Love and pure Truth.

As it has been spoken, there is only one way in which to do this, and that is to commit to the Holy Triads of your being, and to the Diamond Lights within them. Our Diamond Lights therefore wait patiently for the expression of your Diamond Lights, and our Hearts wait patiently for the expansion of your Hearts. For, understand, the Heart of this Universe is your Earth, and the 'H' of your Earth, is the Honour we are asking you to remember and restore to your Hueman experience. For, in Truth, a great Honour has been bestowed upon you, the Honour of full Heart and Soul expression. Allow Honour to become the foundation of your Earth experience. Allow Honour to lead the way, the way of the Heart on Earth, for, you, dear ones, are the very Heart of this Universe. You are the pioneers for the evolution of our Universe, for the evolution of us, the Star Elders, and for the evolution of the Ancient Ones.

So, the Ten Commitments to Self, the Ten Keys to your evolution are the ten ways in which to Honour your Hueman Civilisation, and to re-awaken the very Heart of All Creation, the Heart of God.

We, the Elders of both the Stars and the Planets, wait for this Truth to set you, and us free. For, understand also: we, the Star Elders have been the Guardians of your Hearts, and what you also wish to call your Christ Consciousness, your Central Sun, and your Crystal Connection. But, in Truth, as we are the Guardians of this Christ Consciousness, it is you who are the Activators, and through the activation of your Emotional Beings, the experience of your Hearts, shall the Christ Consciousness, the Central Sun, be re-awakened in this Universe, this Crystal Ball, this Chrysalis of the New World.

As it has been spoken in other Scriptions, there are Five Star Nations who watch over you and witness your evolution, your emotional evolvement back into Love, back into All Existence, and you may call on any of us, at any time. Many of you have already communed with us, consciously or unconsciously, and we wish it to be known that, within your Sacred Southern Cross Star System, a new Council of Star Elders exists. In future Scriptions, there shall be much information available to our Light Channel, 'Starlight', as to what this shall mean to your Earth, your Hearts, and your Huemanity.

We thank you for this time in your space, this moment in your Hearts, for we wait in the wings of your consciousness, we wait for your brave Hearts to flow with the Sacred Waters of Emotion, and to be honoured with every tear and every moment of Joy. For, in the full experience and expression of your emotions, there shall be tears of Joy.

So, hold yourself back no more, for you shall only create sorrow and disease, and know that in your courage, you shall not only awaken yourselves and your Huemanity, you shall also open a Sacred Gateway for your Brothers and Sisters, for your Stars, and for your Planets. With Love, Peace, and with immense gratitude, we, the Star Elders, wait for your call and your commitment.

THE TEN COMMITMENTS

10 I am All with the Mystery of the Goddess, and I am One with the Majesty of God.

9 I am Eternal Spirit.

8 I am in communion with All Creation.

7 I create Infinite Experience.

6 I surrender to my Divine Will.

5 I experience the Light of my Heart.

4 I accept the guidance of my Soul.

3 I honour all my emotions.

2 I nourish my Hueman Temple.

1 I Serve Mother Earth with my gifts.

J
O
Y

ACTIVATION OF
THE TEN COMMITMENTS

As you gaze upon the Ten Commitments, and their placement in your Diamond Light System, we, the Union of Love and Light, we dance in Joy and celebration, for in such a simple intention, and profound commitment, your expansion shall bring such Love and Joy to the Mother and the Father of All Existence, and All Experience.

To assist you in your commitment to Self, we would like to suggest that a daily commitment to your Diamond Lights be experienced and expressed. So, if you choose, speak these Commitments with the commandment of your Divine Will, which also, in essence, is within your Throat Centre.

Feel these Commitments, and be embraced by the gratitude of your Soul and the Joy of your Heart. Know that this Supernova of your consciousness shall radiate its Light through your Experi-mental God Order, the River of Stars shall be birthed within your Diamond Lights, and a grand re-awakening, remembrance, and Re-Union within the mystery and the majesty of your being shall begin.

We would now like to share with you a way in which you may commit to, and expand upon, your individual Gifts of Love and Light. In previous Scriptions we have used the Sacred Equation of your Earth's Birth to assist and guide you with Gifts and Challenges of the Mind, of the Heart and of the Soul, and once again, we wish to use this same Sacred Equation for another purpose. For, understand, your Birthday holds the Sacred Keys to this Light-time of experience, and for the simplicity of the teaching, by creating your own unique Commitments, you will allow your Gifts and Challenges to come into Union. You will allow balance, harmony, and true growth into this, your Light-time, and will open the Gateways to the three Holy Temples of Light within your being.

Author's Note: As a full understanding of this Scription is important, especially for readers not yet exposed to my first channelled work, 'Union - A Guide to the New World', please refer to Appendix B on page 161, as this contains key excerpts from that publication.

So, once again using our channel's Birth Date, the Sacred Equation

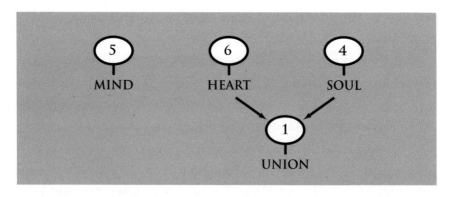

for 23 June 1958 is:

Starlight is a FIVE MIND VIBRATION, and the Fifth Diamond Light is the HEART CENTRE, so the Commitment to assist her with the activation of her Higher Consciousness and its Knowledge would be:-

'Within my Mind, *I experience the Light of my Heart'*.

Starlight is a SIX HEART VIBRATION, and the Sixth Diamond Light is the THROAT CENTRE, so the Commitment to assist her with the activation of the Heart and its expression would be:-

'Within my Heart, *I surrender to my Divine Will'*.

Starlight is a FOUR SOUL VIBRATION and the Fourth Diamond Light is the SOLAR PLEXUS, so the Commitment to assist her with the activation of the Soul and its purpose would be:-

'Within my Soul, *I accept the guidance of my Soul'*.

Starlight is a ONE UNION VIBRATION and the One Diamond Light is the EARTH STAR, so the Commitment to assist her with the activation of her Spiritual essence and its expansion would be:-

'Within my Spirit, *I serve Mother Earth with my gifts'*.

Know your Commitments as Keys to the Gateways of your Diamond Lights, for, as you open your consciousness to the radiant Divinity of these majestic centres, you shall 're-wire', if you choose, your entire mental, emotional, and physical being, and harmony, happiness, and of course, Joy shall be re-awakened within you.

And may we add, 'happiness' is created by your Mind and its perception, which is a truly wonderful experience, however, your Joy is created by your Heart and its Union with your Soul. So, your happiness is like the wind, it breezes in and out of your consciousness, and indeed, enjoy your happiness, by all means, as it is a wonderful tonic for your minds. But, your Joy is Eternal, and is the celebration and pure expression of your very Existence.

THE MEDITATOR

I, Shalamar, now come forth, illuminated by the radiance of your Light. I, Shalamar, now stand before you in reverence and in awe of the Knowledge I perceive within the Temple of your Stars, the Truth I experience within the Temple of your Sun, and the Love that I feel within the Temple of your Moon. For you, dear ones, in perfect reflection, allow me to perceive myself in all *your* beauty, in all *your* mystery, and in all *your* majesty.

I, Shalamar, now bring forth to you a most ancient and pure Truth. It is one that, in its simplicity, and in its serenity, holds the power of All Creation. As with all the individual aspects of energy that have been presented to you within the Union of Love and Light, many perceptions shall have been created with your receiving of these Scriptions. And in Truth, it is your individual and unique essence that allows each of you to perceive us, however you choose.

This, of course, creates the mystery and the magnificence of Eternal Existence, however, I wish to clarify and commit to you, within Holy Communion, the perception of I, Shalamar, that will allow you the Ancient Truth of Self.

I am, in Truth, a Meditator, a Meditator of All Existence, for in All Existence, I am the meditation. I reflect upon and observe; I gaze in peace and serenity; I ponder in silence and solitude; and, in my greatest vision of meditation, I explore the Eternal Bliss of Existence, of its Being, and its Becoming.

And, through my desire and Will, in meditation, I have created my own worlds, my own experiences, my own opportunities for expansion, and I wish it be known now, in pure Truth, that you are also a Meditator, a creator, a ponderer and a peacemaker that creates the worlds within you, and in Truth, around you.

For All Existence only requires one response, and that is the acknowledgement of its very Existence, and within the pure intention of acknowledgement, Existence celebrates itself in JOY. So, to observe, to meditate upon, to ponder and reflect within All Existence, this shall allow All of Existence to expand, to express, and to reflect back upon Itself, All that It Is, and All That It Is Becoming.

And know this: as you are a Meditator, you are also a Master, for a Master creates a concept within their Temple of the Stars, and allows that concept, that Starseed of their Higher Consciousness, to be carried forth upon their emotions, and then will manifest this Starseed within the journey of their Soul. For the Master shall first observe All Existence, and then, through desire of Will, choose what they wish to create and experience and, through action, make it manifest within the worlds of their Being and Becoming.

Understand, as we have shared with you the Truth of the Soul, that the Soul is the dreamer, and this Life is but its dream. Know now that the Soul received its dream through the visions of its Meditator, its Spirit. So the Meditator of your Being is, in Truth, your Divine Source of Self, and the experience of the dream that was received by the Soul then becomes the sacred journey of expression for your Heart.

It is this ancient pure Truth that will set your Hueman Temples free from their 'sleepwalk' and re-awaken them to the Divine dream of the Soul, and the creator of those Divine dreams, the Meditator, the Divine Source of Self which, in Truth, reflects back to you that you are the Divine Source of All Existence.

I, Shalamar, bow before you in reverence, for I, the Meditator, gaze upon my meditation when I gaze upon you. For your Life, in Truth, is a meditation and, shall we say, your Hueman meditations are medications for the Heart, the Soul, and the Mind of your Hueman Temples.

So, to perceive your Light Cycles as meditations of magnificent dreams, of Divine Creation, of Pure Joy, this shall allow the memory of your majesty to be re-awakened within the Light of your becoming, and within the dream of your destiny. For all experience is created by the meditation of the Meditator, the Divine Source of Self.

Remember, all your experiences are expressions of your meditations, of your Light-times. See your breath as meditation, feel your Heart and Soul as meditation, swim in your oceans as meditation, weep your tears as meditation, and sing your songs as meditation. For all these meditations have been created by you, the Meditator, to reawaken the purity, the passion, the purpose, and the Joy of your Being and Becoming.

THE STAR
AND THE STONE

It is our greatest desire to witness your Joy, and your Joy is the desire of every Heart. We, the Union of Love, and we, the Union of Light, in Union with your Hearts, we embrace the Joy of your being. You are, each of you, a desire of grand proportions to the Mother and Father of your Creation.

The Love of the Mother, and the Light of the Father, embrace you in all your experience, in all your experiment, in all your being, and your becoming. Their Hearts wait in anticipation for your Joy, for your Joy is their very Life-Force; your Joy creates their very Existence, and allows the eternal mystery and magnificence of All Existence to become.

And, may we say, the Heart of our channel has been opened beyond her own recognition, and as she received this concluding Scription of Joy, her Heart ached and burned with the Flame of Union. For understand: to allow Joy to be re-birthed within the Sacred Flame of your Heart, and your experience, you must first release the pains and the struggles of the Heart; the disappointments, the betrayals, the disillusionments. And as the Flame of Joy grows within your Hearts, understand, your tears of release are the physical manifestations of your purification, and your innocence.

In your remembrance of your innocence and your purity, you shall then create your Joy, and this shall birth forth your passion and your purpose. Allow the tears from the Flame to fall gently, and with reverence upon your face. For, in this moment, the Mother and the Father of your very Existence shall be felt within your Heart and Soul.

Each of you is of Star and Stone; each of you is of Heaven and Earth; each of you is Divine and Perfect. Allow the radiant Star in your Heart to shine within the Sacred Temple of your being, for each body that walks upon the Sacred Stone of your Earth is, in Truth, that Sacred Stone, and each Heart that shines with the Light of Love, is in Truth, a Star of Heaven. And when there is Union of the Star and the Stone, the Joy of Truth, the Joy of Union, shall explode through every Diamond Light, within you, and around you.

We, the Union of Love, and we, the Union of Light gaze, in awe, upon the kingdom of your Hearts, we gaze in awe upon the beauty of your Temples. We wish you Joy, Peace and Passion, for in Truth, this is what you are.

You are the Peace of your Souls, you are the Passion of your Hearts and, when in Union, you become the Joy of the World. Allow yourselves to see what we see in you, allow yourselves to be what you have always been, for, in Union, we are Eternally One.

Remember Joy, dear Hearts, is the true Journey Of You!

WHEN YOU CAN

SWIM WITH JOY

IN THE SACRED POOL

OF YOUR OWN TEARS,

THEN YOU HAVE

REACHED THE POOL

OF COMPLETION.

GREGORY

APPENDIX A

YOUR TREE OF DIAMONDS

Many of you reading these Scriptions would have some idea of your Chakra Systems, the energy gateways and spirals that are within each and every living thing, including your Earth. They are, in reality, energy centres of pure Love and pure Light, and they are reflected in Union with the energy, the 'Light Force' that is around your bodies; the Divine Force that allowed you to take your first breath, your second and your third, that allows you to feel, to nourish yourselves, and to think for yourselves.

Eastern philosophies place great importance on these energy centres and we wish to agree with them as to the importance of understanding, and coming into Union with them.

We now wish to give these holy centres, that you have traditionally called the Chakras, another name and another purpose, and to share with you an expression that we feel is perfect for you as beings of Love and Light.

We realise how precious, in your world, your Diamonds are and how magnificently they reflect the purity of Light and the beauty of Light. You are all Diamonds; you are all purity and beauty; you are all multi-faceted and you are all precious. For this reason, we wish to call your energy centres 'The Diamond Lights'.

With the description and the map we give you now you shall have Ten points of reference, Ten Diamond Lights, and we shall tell you why.

One of the greatest gifts to your Huemanity was a very simple, but also perfect map which was all encompassing. It was, and is, called the

Tree of Life, or the Kabbalistic Tree, and it is a map of your World, your Universe, and of YOU. It is a blueprint of your Universe and everything within it, including your Angelic Realms, and an understanding of God/Goddess/All That Is.

The Kabbalistic Tree has ten major energy centres or spheres that are represented by your Planets, including your Earth, your Moon, and your Sun. These Planets represent what the Jewish tradition calls the Ten Virtues of God. These Ten Virtues, these Ten Gifts, lie deep within each and every one of you. You are a perfect Holygram of your Universe and your Universe of you, You are One. Many of you may wish to study this Kabbalistic Tree, and all of you who do so will receive something very profound from it.

Many changes, however, are taking place within this map of your Universe and this will be discussed at another time. We shall remain, for the moment, expressing and explaining to you the Ten Diamond Lights that rest in and around you.

Allow us, through our Love for you, to take you on a journey to the most magnificent Universe you will ever experience; the Universe of your being. We now wish to give explanation to each of the Diamond Lights set before you.

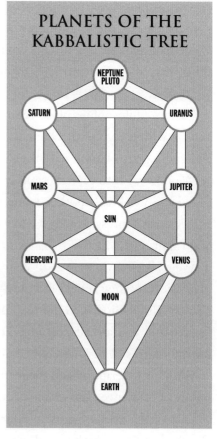

PLANETS OF THE KABBALISTIC TREE

NEPTUNE PLUTO

SATURN   URANUS

MARS   JUPITER

SUN

MERCURY   VENUS

MOON

EARTH

PLANET, NUMBER & SYMBOL ASSOCIATED WITH EACH DIAMOND LIGHT

NEPTUNE & PLUTO	◇	10	CHALICE
URANUS	◇	9	STAR
SATURN	◇	8	DOLPHIN & WHALE
JUPITER	◇	7	CROWN
MARS	◇	6	SWORD
SUN	◇	5	DIAMOND
VENUS	◇	4	ROSE
MERCURY	◇	3	PEARL
MOON	◇	2	WATER
EARTH	◇	1	STONE

THE TEN
DIAMOND LIGHT

We now wish to start at the top of your Hueman Tree, that Universal Tree which has reflected itself in the form of your Hueman body. We shall start with the Diamond Light numbered ONE and ZERO. Some of you may call this your number TEN, however we do wish to place some importance on the unique vibration of each individual symbol that you call numbers.

Many of you know you are your own Divine Creators. Many of you know that what you think comes back to you. Many of you know the power of thought. This One Zero Diamond Light is where it shall manifest, and this One Zero Diamond Light then filters the energy manifested by you down through all the other Diamond Lights.

To break it down even further into another way, your Zero is the most powerful of all your numerical symbols. It represents the unmanifest, the unknown and All That Is. It is an Eternal Circle of pure unknowable Source; it is the Gateway to all Dimensions known and unknown; it represents the Divine Womb of the Great Mother. Everything in your Universe has been birthed from this place of no-thing, this point of the Unmanifest.

Your symbol One represents form, self, ego and complete Union with All That Is. So, understand, from the point of the unmanifest, 'the Zero' is where you place your intentions and your thoughts, and then they are reflected into the One, into the Self.

We suggest, with passion and with purpose that each day, each night, each moment that it comes to your attention, you place Love and Light into this Diamond Centre, for it will surely be reflected through your other Diamond Lights, through your cellular bodies, your emotional and your mental bodies and the bubble in which you find yourself, your auric field. For this One Zero Gateway of Diamond Lights is your direct manifestation of the Eternal Being that you are, and is reflected directly into the Diamond Gateway we have marked as One.

So, in the true sense of the expression, 'As Above So Below', once you understand and embrace the Gateway of the One and the Zero, this will manifest directly into your Earthly experience through the vehicle of your full awareness.

This One Zero Gateway, in your Kabbalistic Tree terms, is now represented by your planets NEPTUNE and PLUTO. Pluto vibrates, in essence, to the Zero and Neptune to the One. The symbol we wish to associate with this Diamond Gateway is the GOLDEN CHALICE of LIFE which you may also term your Holy Grail.

THE NINE
DIAMOND LIGHT

We now bring your attention to the Ninth Diamond Light. NINE to this point has been a number associated with the Universe, associated with completion, and also with the Huemanitarian. As we have said, there are numerous vibrations being expressed by these symbols.

However, apart from the numerical symbol of eight, NINE is the only other symbol to encompass the entire top cube of the Sacred Grid. It contains within it the essence of Heaven (Spirit) and the Sun (Soul) and then extends itself down

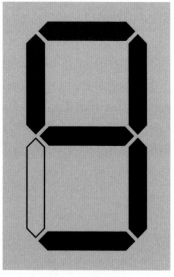

onto the Earth (Service). This explains why it is often called the number of the Huemanitarian, but it also shows the desire of the Divine to birth itself from its Source and become an individual expression (self) to then manifest and experience the Earth Realm.

NINE'S power comes from its direct connection to both Heaven and Earth and the knowledge that by following the Soul's path of service it shall then fulfil its destiny. It is the energy of the TEN which, being the Dark and the Light, the Goddess and the God, the Masculine and the FemiNINE 'birthing' itself into the world of duality, this is the symbol of the NINE.

The planet associated with NINE is URANUS, and the symbol we wish to express this energy with is the STAR, representing the birth of the individual Soul, and creating itself into first form and first light. This is where what you would call your Higher Self, or the Divine expression of your Spirit, resides.

Uranus represents the Will of the Spirit to manifest itself on the Earthly Realm and, in a highly-evolved Soul, this could create an individual of genius and originality. It is also the Gateway of what you would call magic and miracles. With your Hueman consciousness often perceiving magic as the Soul expressing its power of thought and will in a negative way, you often perceive the manifestation of miracles being the Soul expressing its power of thought and will in a positive way. Each and every one of you is capable of creating both magic and miracles, as each and every one of you is capable of creating illusion and Truth.

THE EIGHT
DIAMOND LIGHT

We now bring your attention to another extremely powerful symbol, the Infinite symbol of Love and Light, the symbol you call EIGHT.

It is the focal point, the Gateway, if you choose, between your idea of Heaven and your idea of Earth. It is the Alchemic tool of All Life, of All Thought. As you all well know, your mind can bind you or liberate you. Many of you have been imprisoned by your thoughts, which have kept you from seeing the perfection of your path,

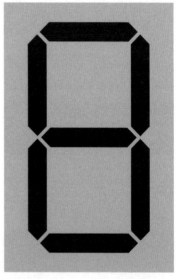

of your lives. We call it the number of Alchemy, for you can transform your lives into perfection or into prisons. As we have expressed in the Scriptions before this, you are Infinite Beings of Love and Light and, if you fail to see the 'Big Picture', many of you would feel trapped on this figure EIGHT.

EIGHT, Infinity and Eternity; these individual expressions of this symbol are what your mind now needs to embrace, so it can have the trust and the faith now required, knowing that all is perfect. Love is perfection; Love is Light; Love uses the vehicle of Light to express its perfection, and you are that Love reflecting that Light in a perfect expression of the life you are now experiencing. Bringing this into your minds will change and transform all your illusions and all your pain back into the perfection of Love it has always been.

For, when you understand the perfection, you will understand there is no right, no wrong, no Karma. All events are neutral events, or even unmanifested events, until you place a thought, a perception on them. A person or an event has no meaning until you place your perception upon it, then, after you've placed your perception upon it through the symbol of this Alchemy, you then create it. From that creation, you then manifest a judgement; whether that judgement binds or liberates, is purely up to you. This is Free Will.

The event has been placed there to reflect a remembrance of 'some kind' to you, a challenge and a gift of 'some kind' to you. It has not been placed there to punish you or congratulate you. This, in your Hueman evolution, will change your perception of Karma. It does not serve you any more.

This is the essence of Alchemy; this is the holy symbol of your EIGHT. This EIGHT is represented by your planet SATURN, and, the symbol we wish to give you is the DOLPHIN and/or the WHALE, for they represent high intelligence, Love and pure communication through their sonar systems and their abode in the great oceans of your Earth, the Waters of All Life, the Divine Womb of the Great Mother Goddess.

THE SEVEN
DIAMOND LIGHT

We bring your attention now to the symbol of your SEVEN. This Diamond Light, this Diamond Gateway, may be found energetically in the centre of your forehead.

The number SEVEN is a very Sacred number in its interpretation through the ages of your history and your many and varied civilisations. It is the source of sight in your physical experience. It is also the source of Spiritual sight, and the most precious tool you have is your imagination, for it is the way 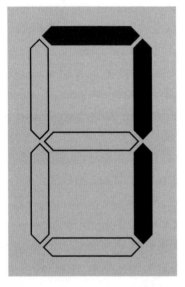 we communicate with you; it is our direct line into your Hueman experience, into your Hueman consciousness.

It is where we present you with symbols and dreams; it is the Divine movie screen of Infinite expressions. It is where you physically expand your consciousness; it is the direct line, if you choose, from Heaven to your Earth through visualisation. It is the centre of the prophet and of the psychic. It is how you perceive things other than your own Hueman realm; it allows the Diamond Light Gateway of God/Goddess All That Is to express itself to you in all its Divine and Sacred forms.

It is represented on the Universal Tree by the planet JUPITER, the planet of expansion, and the symbol we wish to give this Diamond Light of Seven is a CROWN. For you are the ruler and creator of your own kingdom and, in Truth, you are here to love, honour and protect the Sacred Kingdom of your Earth.

Your symbols SEVEN, EIGHT and NINE represent the Upper Triad of your Universal Tree. Symbolically and Spiritually, these three symbols represent your Stars, the first Light seen in your Universe, the first manifestation of Source of Love of All Things.

It is now with great joy and excitement that we bring into your consciousness the Central Triad of your Universal Tree and of your Being. This is the Heart; this is the Central Flame of your very existence in this Hueman Being. It is the grand Union of what you would call your Heaven and what you would call your Earth. It consists of the Numerical Symbols SIX, FIVE and FOUR.

THE SIX
DIAMOND LIGHT

You shall find the Diamond Light of SIX in the region of your throat, the region of your Earthly voice, your expression of all the feelings that reside within your Five symbol and your Four symbol. Structurally speaking, your SIX is the Earthly expression of your self, expressing through your Zero. This is a most powerful Diamond Light indeed for it brings the Union of thought and feeling into Earthly expression.

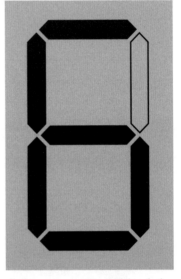

It is the loud speaker, if you choose, of your egos and your Souls. It releases great energy into your energetic field and the energetic field of the Earth Realm. SIX has the ability to bring great Joy and great pain to those who come into range of it, however we would like to add that actions, not words, have the greatest impact.

The SIX represents the physical manifestation of your Free Wills, and we would like to express to you: there are two forms of Will. There is your Free Will, and there is Divine Will, the Will of God/Goddess/All That Is. Also, and make no mistake about this, it is also the Will of your Spirit, which is the purest essence of your Love and Light that placed you here in this Hueman experience, for the purpose of expansion and experience.

This energy of the SIX can bring much conflict to your Hueman experience, as the Diamond Light of Free Will, it can in many ways be in conflict with the Divine Will, or Higher Self, which resides in the NINE vibration. If the SIX, which is your Free Will, was in perfect alignment and Union with the Nine, your Divine Will, it would be brought back into Joy and Love.

Many of you experience much discomfort in the region of your neck, your head and your shoulders because you resist the UNION of the SIX with the NINE. Resistance is over; your Divine Will has placed you here with the experiences you are having for the Grandest Enlightenment and the Grandest Union of Love. You are now being asked to surrender your Free Will so it may rise up back into Union with the Nine, your Divine Will.

From your Universal Tree, the planet that associates itself with the region of your throat is your planet MARS. The symbol we wish to give you for this Diamond Light is the SWORD; the Sword of Truth, the Sword of Surrender, a pure force of Light and right use of Will.

THE FIVE
DIAMOND LIGHT

And if this is not enough for you, we now bring you a most grand vibration of Diamond Light, your Diamond Light of FIVE – the very centre of your Universe and your physical being.

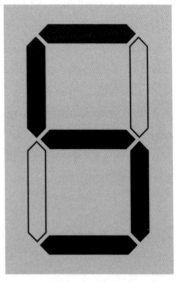

The Diamond Gateway of ALL LOVE, whether it be physical, emotional, Soul or Spirit, this is the crossroads, if you like, the God Spark, the flash point of your manifestation. It is the Flame of Eternal Love, of Light. It is the passion, the pleasure, the purpose; it is where all pain eventually comes to be embraced, to be healed and transformed into more passion, pleasure and purpose. It is hard for us to convey to you what this Central Diamond Light actually is, for as we look into each and every Heart, we are speechless as to the beauty and the power we find there.

Energetically, it is this Diamond Light that fuels and maintains all other Diamond Lights contained within your being, and, make no mistake, within your Universe. It is the nuclear power station of your bodies and, if it is not allowed to freely give its energy to the other centres that it fuels and maintains, it will eventually bring the whole Diamond Light System to shut-down.

As you look symbolically at the sacred grid of the FIVE, you will see that it is in perfect balance with itself. Again, it reflects back on itself; it is nearly a complete Eight, but it has allowed itself to be left open above and below so all energies may come through it and around it to receive its Love. It is the Infinite Symbol of the Eight that has allowed Gateways to open so that energy can move freely around it, above and below it.

For FIVE is at the centre; FIVE is the balance, is the freedom, and freedom is the foundation of All Hearts. The FIVE Diamond Light is represented by your SUN, which gives you life on Earth, which gives you power on Earth.

The only symbol that we know could possibly be placed in this Diamond Light Centre is that of a DIAMOND, for it reflects its Love and its Light to all other Centres. Your Hearts are pure beacons, reflectors and transmitters of Love and Light.

THE FOUR
DIAMOND LIGHT

Four, if seen as a graphic symbol on the Sacred Grid of Eight, will show you an open vessel at the top, with a single One travelling down into the lower region of the Eight. This upper vessel, this cup, is filled with your Spirit and your Divine Will, wishing to bring its Love and its Light to your Earth.

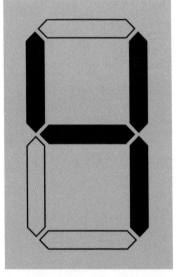

Your FOUR sits in the region of your Solar Plexus, which is the house of your Soul and, as we have said, your Heart reflects the Love and the Light of your Soul, so your Soul is the foundation of all your experience. Your Soul is the compass and your Heart lights your Soul's Way. You are here FOUR a purpose; you are here FOUR experience; you are here FOUR your highest Love; you are here FOUR the purpose of Service.

This Diamond Light, this Gateway for your Soul is a very sensitive place; it is a place of purification, of planning, of personal power. It is the fuel that feeds the fire in your Hearts so that the fire in your Hearts may fuel all the Diamond Lights.

The FOUR Diamond Light is the magnetic fuel that allows the Heart to expand into the depths of your being and be drawn back to the fuel of your Soul. It allows the Spirit to travel around your body and, of course, the figure of your Eight. Your Heart and your Soul, in Union, fuel the fire of your Spiritual experience.

In fact, it is only for the purpose of your understanding that we separate the symbols of the FIVE and the FOUR. If they are brought into Union, they create the NINE – your Higher Self, your Soul Star, your Divine Will, so only for the purpose of these Scriptions do we separate them. However, we wish to say, as part of your evolution, these will, in energy, begin to become One, as they have already in some advanced Souls. So for the purpose of the teaching, we wish to place the planet VENUS in your FOUR Diamond Light, for she is seen as the planet of Love and relationships.

The power of Love in the relationship between your Heart and your Soul is truly a grand one. For the purpose of the teaching, we wish to put the ROSE as the symbol of this centre, for the sweetness and the perfection and the beauty of the Rose is to remind you of the beauty and the Love and the perfection of your own Soul.

THE THREE
DIAMOND LIGHT

This brings us to the Diamond Light that you call THREE. This sits in the region of your abdomen, just below your navel. THREE in your numerical understanding has always been the number of Creation so, of course, it sits in the creative centre of your bodies, which represents energetically the Womb of the Mother, the Light Force of the Father.

It is represented by your planet MERCURY, which traditionally has been the ruler of the mind; however, for

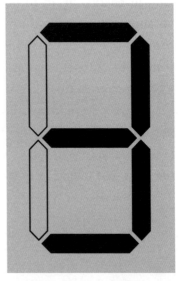

the higher purpose of Union between the mind and body, MERCURY has been placed in your Diamond light of THREE.

Understand this: THREE Centre relates to all your Hueman relationships, your creativity and how you give and how you receive. This is where you first physically manifest your mental and genetic conditioning. Two examples of this purification process would be the menstrual cycle in women and ejaculation in men; it requires creativity to be expressed in whichever form you choose. It is the Hueman home of the creative and the destructive Goddess Energy, whether you be male or female in expression.

This Diamond Light must be honoured for it is the birthplace for other Sacred Souls; it is the Gateway into the Earth plane for other Sacred Souls of Love and Light. You must understand this now if you wish your physical bodies to be in harmony and balance with the evolution of your Souls.

The symbol to best express the vibration of the Diamond Light of THREE is a PEARL, for it is the Pearl of Wisdom, the Pearl of Higher Consciousness being grounded into your Hueman expressions for the purpose of Pure Creation. It is the Gateway of All Births, whether it be an idea, Union with another, or the birth of a Soul. It contains the Divine Waters of I, the Mother, and from a single grain of sand, a single thought, a single seed of light, be it be placed with Love, shall, in Truth, become a Pearl.

THE TWO
DIAMOND LIGHT

I now draw your attention even further into your bodies, to the basement, if you choose, of this Temple of Love and Light that you embody. It is where the foundations of your Temple lie. It is the Diamond Light of TWO. It is the place however, where many of your fears and doubts are placed, as you would place your old unwanted items in the basements of your Hueman homes. It is where I have placed the symbol of your MOON which, in your Kabbalistic teachings, they have called the foundation of the Tree of Life.

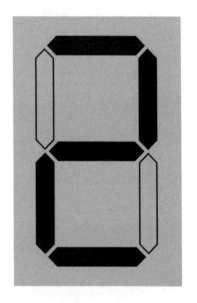

This Diamond Light of TWO is the physical foundation of your bodies, the furnace that fuels the life force for your physical well-being. As many of you know, this energy centre, this Diamond Light Gateway, connects to your renal system just as you know your physical kidneys purify your blood and your blood is your life stream.

It is where the Rainbow Serpent can lie dormant or be activated in your bodies. It is what your Eastern World has called your Kundalini. When this Kundalini, this Rainbow Serpent, is activated, it is I, the Goddess of the Moon, that reaches up to the God, the Sun in your Hearts, for pure Union of pure Love and pure Light.

Take some time in your meditation, feel the rhythm of this base Diamond Light, this foundation of your physical experience. For, when the rising of the Rainbow Serpent from your foundation comes into Union with the Golden Light of the Sun in your Hearts, there is Union, there is complete Union of the Sacred Grid of Eight bringing Infinite Life, Infinite Energy and Infinite Truth.

The explosion of Love and Light expresses itself through your Heart and then sends rays of Sacred Light up into the highest realms of your mind and beyond.

The symbol I wish to give this Diamond Light of TWO, the Gateway of the Rainbow Serpent, is a drop of pure WATER. This is the elixir of Hueman life and it is the manifestation, the lifestream of the Waterfall Way.

THE ONE
DIAMOND LIGHT

The last, but absolutely not the least, of these Diamond Lights is the Diamond Light of ONE.

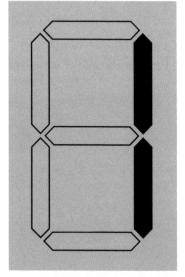

It is hard to be expressed in Hueman terms for it represents All That Is but it is also the individual or singular expression of All That Is. In your Hueman form, you have required this Diamond Light of ONE to be placed in your energetic and magnetic field, for it is the grounding, the gravity, required for you to remain earthed.

It has been placed in your earth so that you may fully experience your physical, emotional and mental expressions. It provides Union with your Earth and Union with the Heart and Soul of your Earth. It is the Diamond Light of your Earthly abundance, for it is where the aura of your being is maintained and created; it is where the unseen bubble of light that you are, is grounded.

It allows you, this Diamond Light of ONE, to experience the illusion of separateness from the rest of your Universe, but it is also the Diamond Light of ONE that brings Union with your Earthly home. It is where the Heart of your Earth can place her beat, so that it may vibrate through your auric field and then make its way into your physical body, bringing Union with the beat of your own Heart. Your Heartbeat may then travel out into your auric body and find Union with that of the Earth.

The ONE Diamond Light is where the Spirit of your Earth and the Spirit of your Soul may come into Union for full expression. For the purpose of the teaching, we wish the Sacred Diamond light of ONE, the Gateway between Earth and Hueman, to be represented by your Planet EARTH, and the symbol we wish to give you now is a STONE. For, understand: the highest purpose of your Soul is to create Union in full consciousness with your STAR and your STONE. For you are the Stars of Light that have travelled long and hard to be in Union with the Sacred Stone of your Earth.

Your Diamond Light of ONE is, in Truth, I, the Mother, who has taken physical form in the expression of your Earth, and it is your Hueman Temples that rest on me that I honour and love, and am more than glad and graced to support. Each and every Heart, each and every Soul shall remember this: Be it *now* or be it in the following moment of *now*, you shall remember, you shall heal, you shall manifest all of who you have always been.

Understand, my dear ones, that the expressions of the Diamond Lights, as we have explained them to you, are only minute aspects of these magnificent Gateways which each of you hold within and around your Hueman Temples. We wish you to perceive this Scription more as an invitation, an opening for your Heart, your Soul and your Mind so that you may begin a truly magnificent journey of Self.

The only boundary you possess for this journey of inner-discovery is your imagination.

We have kept the Scription in simple terms for the very reason that Love and Truth and Light reflects its beauty in its very simplicity. Your days of chaos and conflict are drawing very quickly to an end, and for some, this is already the case.

Your Diamond Lights wait in much anticipation for your company and for your exploration. They have been placed within you by the Divine, for you are Divine, and our only request is your Remembrance of the Truth, for it is the only Gateway to Love and Joy and Freedom of the Heart and Soul. You are deserving of this or you would not be in Hueman form. You will discover, through a very simple and beautiful process, the Gifts and Challenges that your Soul has chosen for itself in the journey of Remembrance of your Divine Love and your Divine Light.

With Love from I, the Mother, I now invite you to explore and express all of who you are and are Infinitely Becoming.

APPENDIX B

THE SACRED EQUATION

It is now that we ask you to receive the Sacred Formula of your Souls. The equation for Knowledge, Truth and the experience of Love are all within your date of Earth Birth. Understand that the Love of The Mother and the Truth of The Father are the creators of the Child Knowledge.

As you have already been told, you are all Father, Mother and Child. The Sacred numerals of your birth date are your key to that Love, that Truth and that Knowledge.

As we have previously expressed, all the teachings of your numerals to this point are true and correct, and also as we have expressed, everything is in the process of expansion, so new ideas, new equations and new expressions are being birthed here and now, in your space and time.

We wish to divide this Sacred Equation of your Earth Birth into Three Aspects, and these three aspects will show you the Holy Trinity that lies within each and every Hueman Being.

Each aspect of this Holy Trinity is, in essence, a Spiritual Temple of Light, and these Temples of Light exist in the Three Triads of Diamond Lights within your bodies. These three Temples of Light are also represented by the Central Pillar of your Tree of Life.

THE THREE TEMPLES OF THE DIAMOND LIGHT SYSTEM

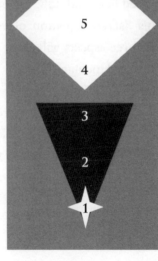

TEMPLE OF THE STARS

STARS
FIRST LIGHT
KNOWLEDGE

TEMPLE OF THE SUN

SUN
CENTRAL FLAME
TRUTH

TEMPLE OF THE MOON

MOON
DIVINE REFLECTION
LOVE

THREE TEMPLES OF LIGHT, THE STARS, THE SUN & THE MOON

Each Temple of Light represents the DAY, MONTH or YEAR of your Earth Birth.

THE DAY YOU ARE BORN resonates within your Temple of Starlight, where all aspects of the Soul's mind and memory are created and put into thought-form by the Soul. So your DAY numeral represents the MIND, and the individual identity or ego, the Soul has chosen for a life cycle, so it may experience KNOWLEDGE.

THE MONTH YOU ARE BORN resonates in your Temple of Sunlight, where all aspects of the Soul's heart and desires are put into emotional form by the Soul. So the MONTH numeral represents the HEART, and the individual expression the Soul has chosen for a life cycle, so it may experience TRUTH.

THE YEAR YOU ARE BORN (not the century) resonates in your Temple of Moonlight where all aspects of the Soul's reflection and cycles are created and put into action by the Soul. So your YEAR numeral represents the SOUL, and the individual purpose the Soul has chosen for a life cycle, so it may experience LOVE.

We wish to express that in the YEAR you were born, that you only use the last two digits of your birthday. For understand: the CENTURY in which you are born is the "playing field", if you choose, that your Soul has wished to come in on, to express itself.

THE CENTURY OF UNION

The Century in which you are born is the energetic vibration the Earth and the Souls upon her wish to endure and wish to expand upon as a GROUP SOUL.

So understand: to take this a step further, your 20th Century, your Nineteen Hundreds, is the vibration in which all of you, in communion with these Scriptions, have birthed yourselves. It was a Century of discovery between the Self and the Universe, with the One being the Self, the Nine being the Universe.

You travelled long and hard in those one hundred years, discovering more about the Self, but also the world around you and the Universe in which you live. You created satellites, and you are sending shuttles to spaces never before dreamt of by man. And, in that expansion and that expression of wishing to experience your Universe in your last quarter of that century, you also, with intensity, went within, through your self exploration, through your workshops and through your self inquiry.

It was a Century of extremes. It was a Century of exploration. It was a Century of enormous freedom and enormous restriction. All Souls that earthed themselves in that playing field of the 20th Century came for dynamic expansion of one form or another. And understand your 1900's, the One and the Nine, when in Union (added together), come back to the ONE, come back to the Self. This has been a very important part of the Soul's journey, however now the Soul is being asked to leap into Union with your "2000". For understand: two is partnership, two is Union, and as we have shown you, Two is the Goddess.

You are now in the middle of a great tidal change, a wave of huge proportions. You cannot resist this Wave or this Waterfall Way. So the "playing field" has changed and the "ground rules", if you choose, are also in the process of changing. You are now here for the Soul to experience Union. You are the Holy Trinity, you are the Mother, the Father and the Child. You are the Mind, the Heart and the Soul of the One Source. So the DAY you are born will reflect the gifts and challenges of your MIND. The MONTH you are born will reflect the gifts and challenges of your HEART, and The YEAR of the Century you are born in will reflect the gifts and challenges of your SOUL.

To simplify this even further, as we set before you the gifts and the challenges of each sacred number of your Earth Birth, we wish to give the gift and the challenge of the Heart and Soul in two ways. An example would be: if the Month number you were born was a three, the month of March, you would refer to the Three Gift Vibration as guidance for your HEART, or the emotional gift and challenge of this life cycle.

And if the YEAR you were born was a Five, you would refer to the Five Gift Vibration for the gift and challenge of your Soul's chosen purpose.

However, as we have said, all is coming back into Union, your Heart and Soul are coming back into Union. So, if you choose, you could add the Three Heart and the Five Soul to bring it into what we would like to express as an Eight Union or HOUL Vibration.

Again, with purpose and passion, we "play" with your words. Union of the Heart with the Soul brings your Spiritual expression into Hueman Houliness, or the Heart Of Unconditional Love.

HEART
OF
UNCONDITIONAL
LOVE

So you may approach this Sacred equation in two ways, for understand, each of you are All these gifts and All these challenges, no matter what your Earth Birth numerals. We are just putting before you the individual expressions which your Mind, your Heart and your Soul have come to experience.

The information, however in all the gift vibrations, will also bring much knowledge to each individual.

The DAY you are born, the Soul's Mind expression, we wish to keep in extreme simplicity. For the benefit of the mind, we have put before you a simple chart stating the gift and the challenge.

This diagram also associates with the Heart and Soul vibrations, and we have given detailed information about these because they relate to the very Heart and Soul of the teaching.

The mind only needs one word to then create a thousand words, a thousand thoughts and a thousand visions.

So, we do not wish to hinder the experience of the Heart and the Soul with the complexities of the Mind, for your mind will still have to digest and clarify the information given in relation to the Heart and the Soul. So the mind's gift and challenge are being expressed in the utmost simplicity.

You may wish to also use your traditional numerology to play with and explore the information set before you now, for you shall still find truth and knowledge with any formula you choose to use.

Remember, you are the Divine Creators and we are only putting before you the tools and the material to create whatever you choose yourselves to be.

This information of your Sacred Equation is for the Divine purpose of Love and Truth and Knowledge. For, just as your Souls have been birthed from Love and Truth, understand, you are the child of Knowledge, and all that Knowledge, Love and Truth may be remembered through the Sacred Numbers of your Earth Birth.

A SACRED
EQUATION EXAMPLE

We wish to share with you a more detailed example of a Sacred Equation and our "channel" has kindly offered her "Earth Birth" for this process. In love and laughter, we kindly thank Starlight's Ego for allowing us to disclose such information.

The Sacred Equation for 23 June 1958 is:

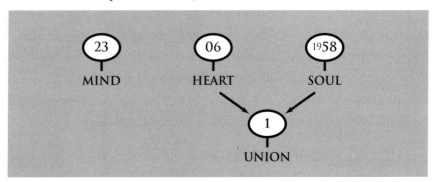

You always add the numbers until you arrive at a single digit. This also applies to what you traditionally call your Master numbers or double symbol numerals; eg 11, 22, 33, etc.

It does mean, however, that the intensity of the single digit would be amplified in the Soul's experience of the gift and challenge. A "10" symbol would reduce back to the One, (as zero is the un-manifest).

So Starlight arrived at her Earth Birth with a:

FIVE MIND VIBRATION	SIX HEART VIBRATION
FOUR SOUL VIBRATION	ONE UNION VIBRATION

THE FIVE MIND VIBRATION gives Starlight the gift to transform information for others – hence her channelling abilities, but alas, her challenge is the need for constant confirmation mentally of the information she receives, whether it be from us the Union, or her fellow hueman beings. So the receiving of these Scriptions has given her and us the opportunity to enhance her gift and transform her challenge.

THE SIX HEART VIBRATION gives Starlight the gift to express the truth to others and to express information for Spirit, however her challenge has been to emotionally surrender, not resist, her own Divine Will, and be able to speak her own truth. So through surrender, her Heart is then allowed to experience being of Service which, in return, gives her emotional nourishment and security.

THE FOUR SOUL VIBRATION gives Starlight the gift to inspire others to get in touch with their own Souls Journey and respond to their abilities (hence these Scriptions!), however the challenge for her is to nurture and support herself, and not fall into the trap of self-criticism. For, to allow the passion and purpose of her Soul to be expressed, will bring her the inner love and acceptance desired by all Souls.

THE ONE UNION VIBRATION would allow the highest purpose of Starlight's heart and soul to be expressed, which is the grounding of heaven on earth. And in love and truth, long before these Scriptions were received by her, we could feel her longing to be given exactly that, the experience of Heaven on Earth.

With the Union Vibration, no challenge exists in the experience as your Heart and Soul are in Union and expressing fully their highest purpose.

Each and every Heart and Soul is now on the journey to that very Union, and each and every Union will see the Heart and Soul return to the full experience and expression of its 'Houliness'.

THE HUEMAN PATH OF UNION

SPIRITUAL GIFT	DIAMOND LIGHT	HUEMAN CHALLENGE
THE UNMANIFEST	10	CREATION
OBSERVATION	9	CONTAMINATION
INTEGRATION	8	CONDEMNATION
REALIZATION	7	ILLUSION
SURRENDER	6	RESISTANCE
TRANSFORMATION	5	CONFIRMATION
RESPONSIBILITY	4	PERSECUTION
INITIATION	3	CONFUSION
FOUNDATION	2	DESTRUCTION
UNIFICATION	1	SEPARATION

THE AUTHOR OF 'UNION' AND 'JOY'

Jennifer Starlight, spiritual medium and teacher, is the mother of two teenage children and is a resident of the Gold Coast in Queensland, Australia.

Following publication of 'Joy', Jennifer will present these powerful and unique teachings at 'Communion' Workshops. The gatherings will provide further illumination and understanding of the 'Union of Love and Light' teachings, including the sacred knowledge, charts and exercises, and the individual soul's gifts and challenges for the journey ahead.

As Jennifer continues to receive new teachings from the 'Union of Love and Light' for further publications, these will progressively be included in her Communion Workshops.

Jennifer will also be available for appropriate speaking engagements or other personal appearances.

Jennifer Starlight

For further information including dates and locations of Communion Workshops contact Jennifer Starlight or the publishers at: starlight23@bigpond.com
joshuabooks@bigpond.com

NOTES

NOTES

NOTES

NOTES

NOTES

NOTES